Author: Fiona Macdonald studied History at the University of Cambridge and at the University of East Anglia. She has taught in adult education and in schools and universities, and is the author of bestselling history and fiction books for young readers.

Artist: David Antram studied at Eastbourne College of Art and then worked in advertizing for fifteen years before becoming a full-time artist. He has since illustrated many popular information books for children and young adults, including more than 60 titles in the bestselling *You Wouldn't Want To Be* series.

Editor: Nick Pierce

Additional artwork: Mark Bergin, Giovanni Caselli, Nick Hewetson, Pam Hewetson, John James, Clyde Pearson, Carolyn Scrace

Additional content: Victoria England, Carolyn Franklin, Nick Pierce, Jim Pipe, David Stewart

PAPER FROM

SUSTAINABLE
FORESTS

Published in MMXVIII by
Scribo, an imprint of
The Salariya Book Company Ltd
25 Marlborough Place, Brighton BN1 1UB
www.salariya.com

PB ISBN: 978-1-912233-67-0

SCRIBO   BOOK HOUSE   SCRIBBLERS

1 3 5 7 9 8 6 4 2

Printed and bound in China.

Visit
www.salariya.com
for our online catalogue and
free fun stuff.

The BIG Scream!

The 100 Creepiest, Most Disgusting, Horrifying Things You Should Know

Written by
fiona Macdonald

Illustrated by
David Antram

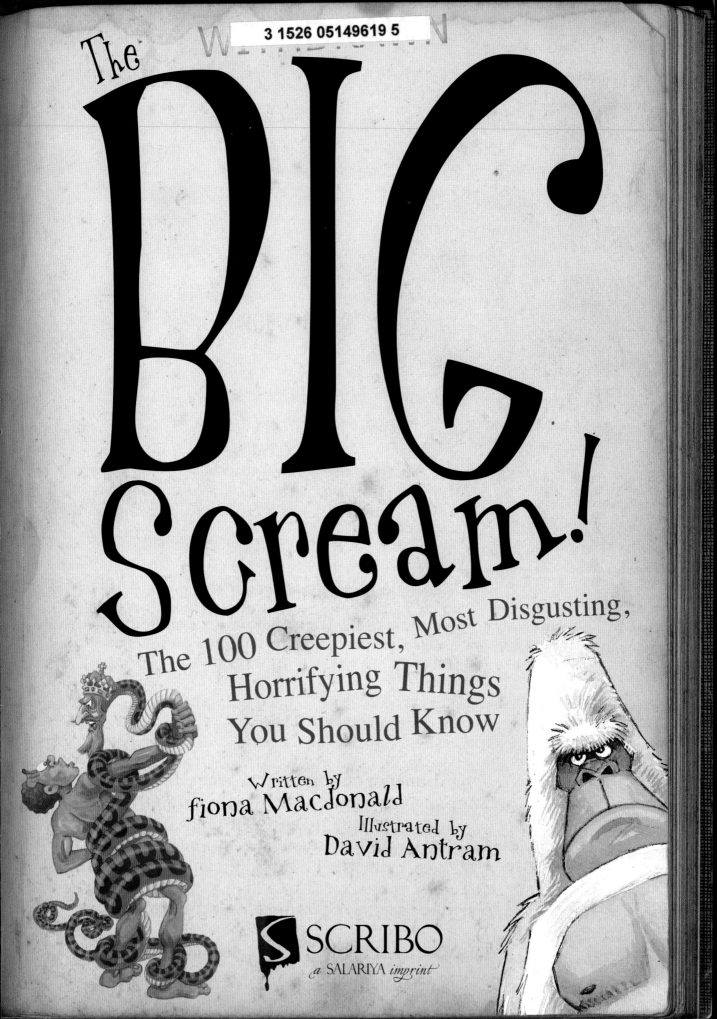

SCRIBO
a SALARIYA imprint

CONTENTS

CONTENTS

The Big Scream!

Introduction

In every book shop, in every library, there are books waiting with quiet menace for an unsuspecting child to open and gasp in fright at the ghastly horrors contained within.

This is one such book...

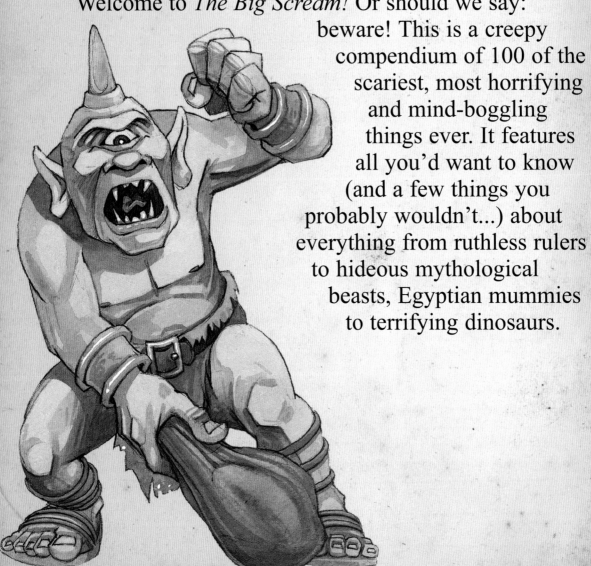

Welcome to *The Big Scream!* Or should we say: beware! This is a creepy compendium of 100 of the scariest, most horrifying and mind-boggling things ever. It features all you'd want to know (and a few things you probably wouldn't...) about everything from ruthless rulers to hideous mythological beasts, Egyptian mummies to terrifying dinosaurs.

Every entry features a brief introduction to the subject, fearsome facts and vital statistics such as names, dates, places and sizes. The book is designed to be dipped into and explored as you see fit, so don't feel the need to read it all at once from cover to cover. Use the introduction to find a subject you're particularly fascinated by and go straight to it.

So what are you waiting for? Take a deep breath, calm your nerves, turn the page and venture inside *The Big Scream!*

...If you dare!

World Map

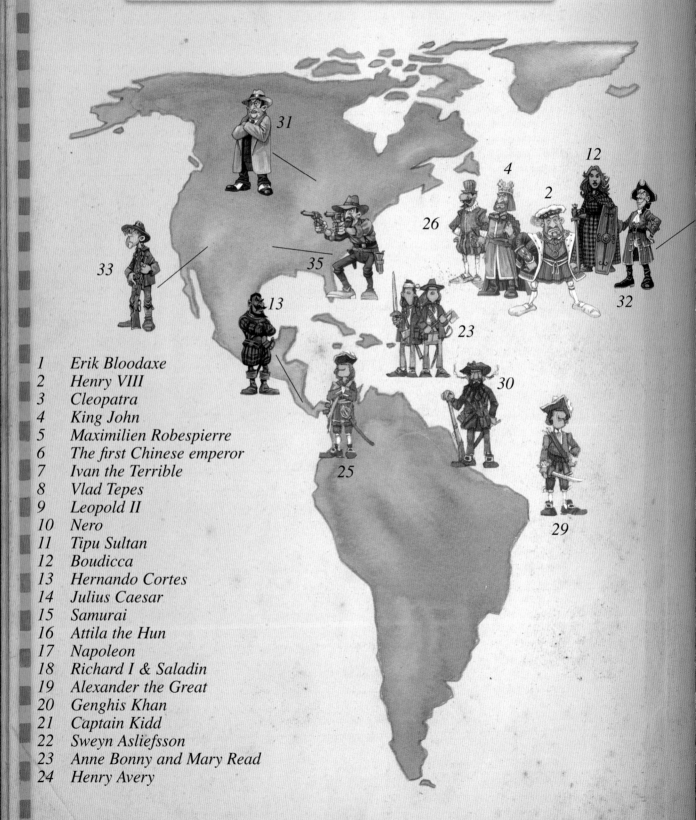

1   Erik Bloodaxe
2   Henry VIII
3   Cleopatra
4   King John
5   Maximilien Robespierre
6   The first Chinese emperor
7   Ivan the Terrible
8   Vlad Tepes
9   Leopold II
10 Nero
11 Tipu Sultan
12 Boudicca
13 Hernando Cortes
14 Julius Caesar
15 Samurai
16 Attila the Hun
17 Napoleon
18 Richard I & Saladin
19 Alexander the Great
20 Genghis Khan
21 Captain Kidd
22 Sweyn Asliefsson
23 Anne Bonny and Mary Read
24 Henry Avery

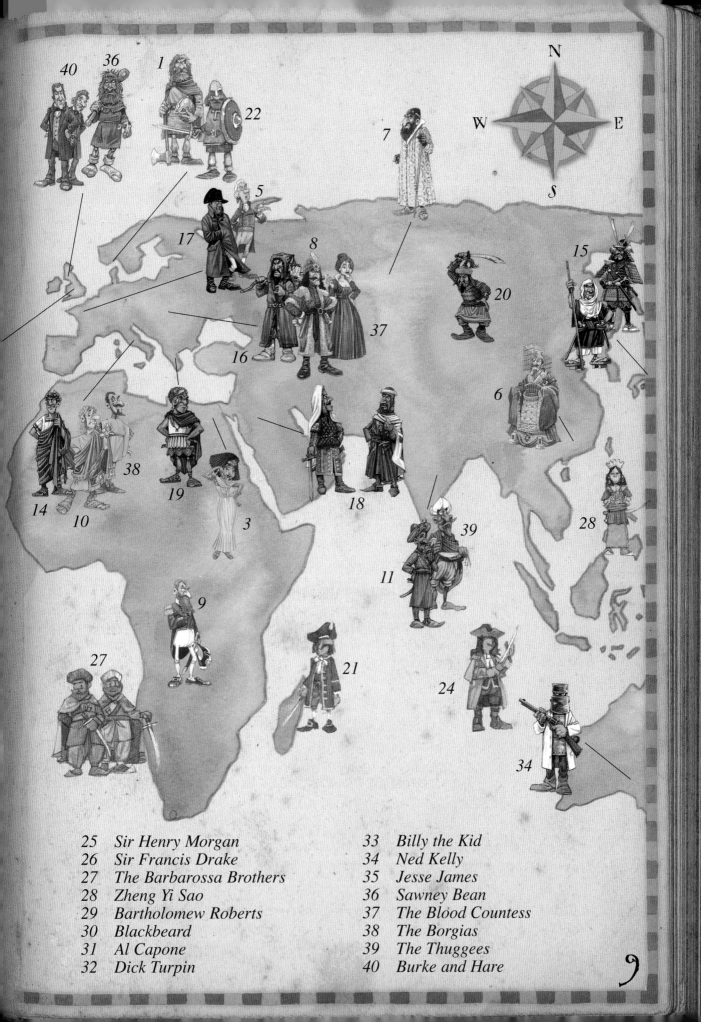

25 Sir Henry Morgan
26 Sir Francis Drake
27 The Barbarossa Brothers
28 Zheng Yi Sao
29 Bartholomew Roberts
30 Blackbeard
31 Al Capone
32 Dick Turpin

33 Billy the Kid
34 Ned Kelly
35 Jesse James
36 Sawney Bean
37 The Blood Countess
38 The Borgias
39 The Thuggees
40 Burke and Hare

9

Awful Ancient Civilisations

Volcanic eruptions, dangerous Olympic events and embalming in Ancient Egypt. Warning: reading this section might make you want your mummy...

The Big Scream!

No 1

food and famine in Ancient Egypt

In very poor families, the diet of bread, beans, onions and green vegetables would have probably become extremely boring. The really poor lived on boiled papyrus roots. Many exotic fruits that we enjoy today, such as lemons and cherries, were unknown.

Tomb offerings

It was the duty of relatives to visit tombs with gifts of food so that the dead person did not go hungry in the afterlife. In a nobleman's tomb at Saqqarah researchers found a whole meal, consisting of barley porridge, quail, kidneys, pigeon stew, fish, a rib of beef, bread and figs.

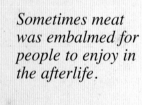

Sometimes meat was embalmed for people to enjoy in the afterlife.

Nice to meat you

Egyptians enjoyed beef most, if they could afford it. It was expensive because cattle needed fields of grass to eat and that took up precious land. People thought that mutton and goat were not so good, and pork and fish were considered unclean.

Gulp!

How to make fire

It took a bow-drill, a piece of wood with a row of holes, and a hard stick that just fitted into them. The stick was pressed into a hole and rotated fast with the drill. As the wood rubbed together, a spark was produced.

Worn gnashers

Most Egyptians had terrible teeth, as sand from the desert got into their bread and ground their teeth down. The Egyptians cleaned their teeth with toothbrushes made from twigs and toothpaste made from natron, a natural salt found on the shores of the desert lakes.

Owww!

What did the wealthy eat?

Even prosperous peasants had their own vegetable patches. Pigeons, crane, teal, geese and ducks were reared for eating and food was forced into some birds to fatten them. Food was bought at the local market where country people sold what they did not need for themselves. As well as growing and buying, people hunted and fished for food; this was a way for poor people to get delicacies.

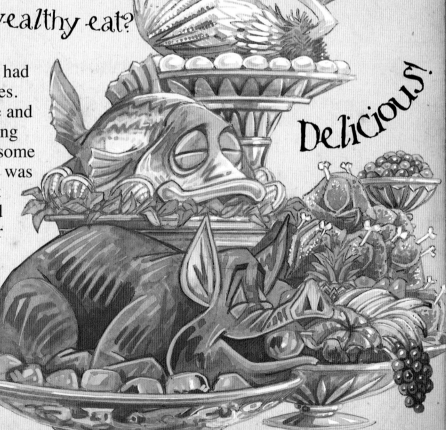

Delicious!

Dinner-party plates were encrusted with jewels.

The Big Scream!

№ 2

Crime and punishment in Ancient Egypt

No-one was more important than the pharaoh. His Egyptian subjects were anxious for his welfare and keen to obey him. He was all-powerful, all-knowing, and ruled everyone's fate. He ruled the government and law courts, was chief priest of the temples, headed the army and controlled trade, irrigation, mines and granaries.

Ask the statue

If a crime couldn't be proven in court, the victim could appeal to a local god when its statue was paraded through town. They could call out their problem to the statue – 'Lord, who stole my ox?' or, 'Who has moved my boundary stones?' and the statue might nod at the thief's door.

A taxing time

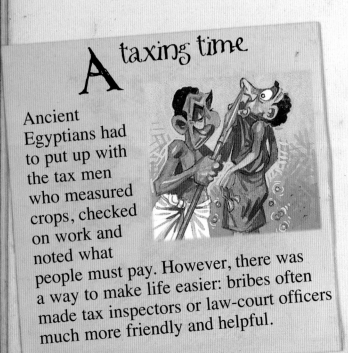

Ancient Egyptians had to put up with the tax men who measured crops, checked on work and noted what people must pay. However, there was a way to make life easier: bribes often made tax inspectors or law-court officers much more friendly and helpful.

Punishments

Beating was the most common punishment. Slaves, servants and hard-up taxpayers were beaten as much as their punishers liked, but if a court ordered a beating, the weapon and the number of blows would be stated.

Smack!

Be prepared!
Always expect the very worst

Tomb robbery!

Every Egyptian pharaoh and his officials feared that the treasures in their tomb would be targeted by robbers. And they were right: few tombs escaped this unwanted attention. Robbers ripped open the mummies, looking for treasure, so they often had to be re-wrapped, sometimes gaining extra heads or legs in the process!

The penalty for tomb robbing was torture and then a slow and painful death by impalement.

Hieroglyph for impalement

What were they looking for?

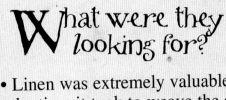

- Linen was extremely valuable because of the time it took to weave the smallest amount. It could also be re-used.

- Glass was scarce in ancient Egypt. Since it could be melted down and made into new objects, stolen glass could not be traced.

- Gold from jewellery was prized and melted down to re-use.

- Frankincense and myrrh were highly prized because of their fragrance and their use in the art of mummification.

The Big Scream!

№ 3

Hard labour

Most people in ancient Egypt faced a life of hard work. The pharaoh sent officials around the villages to call people up to build pyramids. It took 20 years and a workforce of 4,000 to build one stone pyramid. The men worked from sunrise to sunset, slept in crowded barracks and only got one day off in ten. There was no machinery, so workers had to haul the building materials manually and were often involved in serious accidents.

Heave-ho!

The pyramid of power

Here is an overview of the power structure in ancient Egypt, with the most powerful at the top:

The Pharaoh
The Great Royal Wife
Members of the Royal Family
The Vizier
Noblemen
Army Officers
Court Officials
Priests and Priestesses, Doctors
Scribes and Teachers
Artists
Craftsmen
Foot Soldiers
Fishermen and Farmers
Labourers, Tomb Builders

Ouch!

Be prepared!
Always expect the very worst

Sent to the quarries

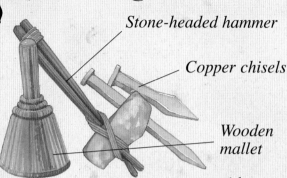

Stone-headed hammer

Copper chisels

Wooden mallet

Most workers sent to quarries would be working underground, as the best stone was beneath the surface. It was backbreaking work, but not as grim as being sent to quarry granite in the far south of Egypt. It was boiling hot there and workers would be out in the open, trying to cut into very hard rock with a lump of stone.

Working on the farm

Some people in Egypt were very rich – the pharaoh and his court, high-ranking officials and wealthy landowners – but the majority were poor. Some made a living by making things to sell, especially in the towns, but most people earned their keep by farming the land. Ordinary Egyptians grew crops for rich landowners; in return they were allowed a patch of land to grow things to feed their own family.

Careful! *Careful!*

Scraping a living

For eight months farmers were hard at it, ploughing, sowing, weeding, watering (it hardly ever rained) and harvesting. Then the Nile flood came and for the rest of the year they couldn't farm, because the land was under water.

Mattock

 **4**

Mummification

The ancient Egyptians took a lot of trouble getting ready for life in the next world. Those who could afford to do so made elaborate preparations. Ordering a tomb built of stone was the first step. All wealthy people did this long before they expected to die. They might also arrange the details of their own mummification, to make sure they were given the best.

Gory mummification

The brain was removed first, pulled out through the nostrils with an iron hook. Then a long cut was made on the left side of the body through which all the internal organs were removed.

Urgh!

Boo!

A priest dressed as the god Anubis supervised the wrapping.

Be prepared!
Always expect the very worst

Get stuffed!

The heart was left inside the body which was then put in natron to dry out for 100 days. After this, the skin was shrivelled and wrinkled and the body looked like a piece of old leather. The empty space where the organs were was filled with sawdust, rags and chaff. False eyes were made out of onions and sometimes false hair was made from string.

Canopic jars

The canopic jar with the head of the god Imsety contained the liver.

The jar with the jackal head of Duamutef contained the stomach.

The intestines were put in the jar topped with the hawk head of the god Qebehsenuef.

The jar topped with the god Hapy contained the lungs.

Making the mummy

It took 15 days and 20 layers of linen bandages to wrap up the mummy. Resin was used to glue the bandages together. Linen pads were placed between the bandages to give a good rounded shape. Once completely wrapped in bandages, the mummy was placed in two special large shrouds secured with linen strips.

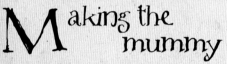

In the afterlife

In death non-royals were judged before Osiris and their hearts weighed against the Feather of Truth. If found free from sin, the deceased would be admitted to the realms of the dead. The monster Ammut (a combination of crocodile, lion and hippo) waited in the judgement hall to eat the hearts of those that failed the test.

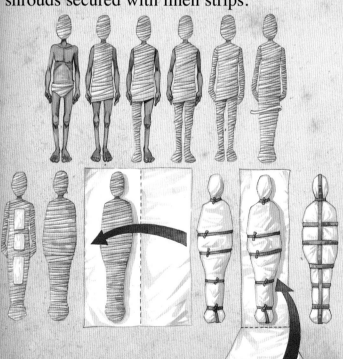

19

N⦾ 5

Ginger, the first Egyptian mummy

Nicknamed 'Ginger' because of his red hair, he was discovered buried in sand in Gebelein in Egypt. Dating from around 3400 BC, his body was mummified naturally by the hot and very dry sand that absorbed all the moisture in it. Ginger is ancient Egypt's earliest known mummified body.

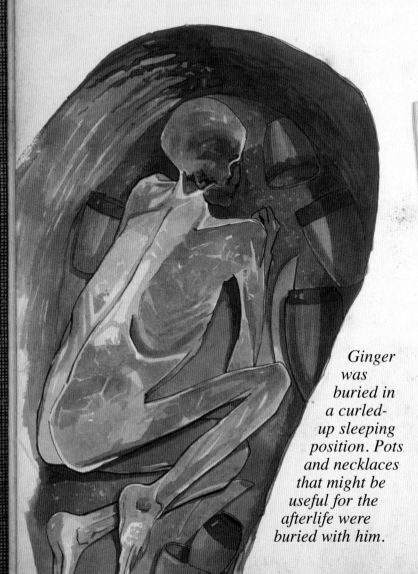

Ginger was buried in a curled-up sleeping position. Pots and necklaces that might be useful for the afterlife were buried with him.

Vital statistics

Name: 'Ginger'
Discovered: Gebelein, Egypt
Original burial: c.3400 BC
Current location: British Museum, London, England

You wouldn't want to know this:

Ginger has been in the British Museum in London for more than 100 years. The temperature in the museum is causing Ginger's skin to peel off. The museum's scientists have tried to glue it back on.

Be prepared!
Always expect the very worst

Ötzi the Iceman

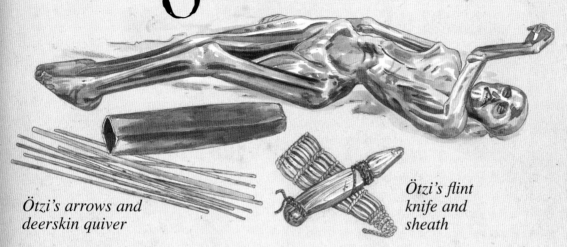

*Ötzi's arrows and
deerskin quiver*

*Ötzi's flint
knife and
sheath*

Ötzi the Iceman is Europe's oldest mummy, found in September 1991. He dates from the same period as Ginger. Ötzi's nickname comes from the Ötztal Alps where he was found, on the border between Italy and Austria. When bodies are embalmed, their soft parts rot; but Ötzi was naturally mummified by freezing, which preserved his human appearance.

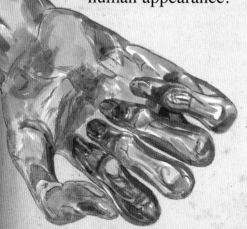

Basket burial

This Egyptian skeleton from 5200 BC, buried in a basket and interred in a tomb, rotted in the normal way. But other bodies buried in hot, dry sand were naturally dried out and preserved. It did not take the ancient Egyptians long to realise that removing fluid from a corpse aided the preservation process.

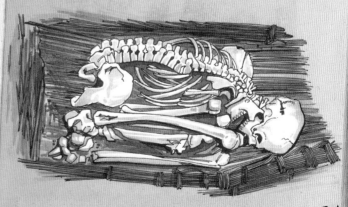

Ötzi's neatly clipped fingernails, his insulated clothing and his rucksack holding supplies caused his corpse to be mistaken for a recent death when it was first found.

The Big Scream!

No 6

Tutankhamun

The almost intact tomb of Tutankhamun – the most famous mummy of all time – was discovered in the Valley of the Kings by archaeologist Howard Carter in 1922. Tutankhamun is not a particularly scary-looking mummy – what's more scary is how he was treated by Howard Carter. And, of course, there is the dreaded curse…

Vital statistics

Name: Tutankhamun
Discovered: Valley of the Kings, Egypt

Original burial: 1324 BC
Current location: Egyptian Museum, Cairo, Egypt

You wouldn't want to know this:

Poor Tutankhamun suffered from a cleft palate, a club foot and various long-term illnesses. He broke his leg shortly before his death – but he probably died of malaria.

Be prepared!
Always expect the very worst

Overdone

So much oil was used in the mummification process that Tutankhamun's flesh stuck to the inside of his coffin. Howard Carter used hot knives to cut up the mummy in order to remove it. The young king's ribs and some other bits are still missing.

Pharaoh's curse?

Lord Carnarvon paid for the archaeological digs which led to the discovery of Tutankhamun's tomb. He died from an infected mosquito bite, four months after the opening of the tomb. Was his death King Tut's revenge? Some people thought so! Yet Howard Carter, who was also present at the opening, lived for a further 17 years.

Poked and prodded

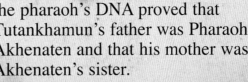

In January 2005, Egyptian researchers carried out a CT scan that produced 1,700 images of the mummy. They found that Tutankhamun's left thighbone had been fractured and that the pharaoh's leg became severely infected just before his death.

In Feburary 2010, a study of the pharaoh's DNA proved that Tutankhamun's father was Pharaoh Akhenaten and that his mother was Akhenaten's sister.

№ 9

Queen Henuttawy

Queen Henuttawy's mummy was painted yellow. To improve her appearance, her lips and cheeks were painted red and her face was packed with a mixture of fat and soda to restore its fullness. She wears a wig made of strands of black string.

Vital statistics

Name: Henuttawy
Discovered: Thebes, near Luxor, Egypt
Original burial: c.1050 BC
Current location: Egyptian Museum, Cairo, Egypt

You wouldn't want to know this:

The embalmers overdid the stuffing on Queen Henuttawy's cheeks and it burst through her skin.

Looking her best

Black string hair

Traces of rouge

Stuffing

Queen Henuttawy was the most important wife of Pinedjem I, Great Priest of Thebes, who ruled Upper Egypt from 1070 to 1032 BC.

Be prepared!
Always expect the very worst

Missing parts

Henuttawy was not the only ancient Egyptian to suffer at the hands of careless embalmers. One mummy's intestines were replaced with a rope. In another, a liver made of cow skin and other organs made from leather and rags were inserted.

Manchester Museum in England has a mummy whose internal organs and legs are missing. Wooden legs had been substituted under the bandages.

Artistic touches

Some embalmers took enormous care to create a lifelike body. The shape was improved by adding linen pads, earth, sawdust and extra bandaging. The skin was coloured red for men and yellow for women. False eyes of glass or stone made the mummy look particularly lifelike.

Shabti

Shabti are small figures placed amongst the grave goods in ancient Egyptian tombs. This one was found in the tomb of Henuttawy. If the queen was called upon to work in the afterlife, the shabti would do the work in her place.

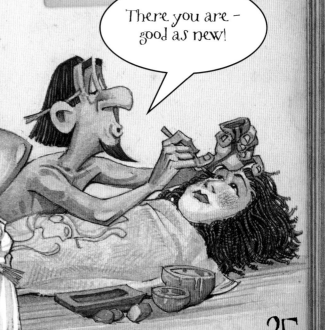

There you are – good as new!

Animal mummies

Animals, like human beings, have also been preserved by accident or design. Fossils provide evidence of tiny creatures from the first phase of life on Earth. Fossils are not mummies, however, since they mostly consist of minerals that have penetrated and replaced the body.

The Egyptians mummified animals as well as humans. Fakes were sometimes made to sell to tourists, in both ancient and modern times.

Vital statistics

Name: Animal mummies

Discovered: Many places in Egypt

Current location: Egyptian Museum, Cairo, and other museums

You wouldn't want to know this:

Some mummies of sacred bulls contain only the head of the animal. What happened to the rest? Some experts think the priests cooked and ate the meat, then mummified the leftovers.

It takes guts to do this job properly, lad.

Sacred animals

The ancient Egyptians believed that some animals were sacred to a particular god. Mummies of that animal would be kept at the god's temple. Crocodiles were sacred to the god Sobek, cats to the goddess Bastet, baboons and ibises to the god Thoth.

101 uses

When European explorers first discovered Egyptian mummies, they did not always treat them with respect. They used them to make medicines, paints, fertiliser, and even torches.

Life after death

Some animals were mummified to provide food for the dead person in the afterlife. Others may have been pets to keep the dead person company. In later times, when Egypt was ruled by the Romans, animal mummies were given as gifts to the gods. They may have been bred specially.

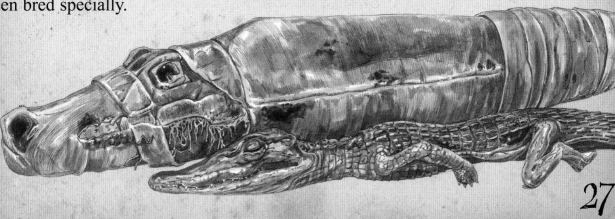

№ 9

Queen Nodjmet

The embalmers of Queen Nodjmet's time were trying out new techniques, using padding, wax and cosmetics to make the mummy more lifelike. Queen Nodjmet's mouth was packed with sawdust and her nose filled with resin. She had artificial eyes made of precious stones, and eyebrows made from real hair. A wig was added to conceal the queen's sparse grey hair and restore her youthful appearance.

Vital statistics

Name: Nodjmet
Discovered: Thebes, Egypt
Original burial: c.1080 BC
Current location: Egyptian Museum, Cairo, Egypt

You wouldn't want to know this:

Nodjmet's face was badly scarred when tomb robbers cut through her wrappings in search of valuable jewellery.

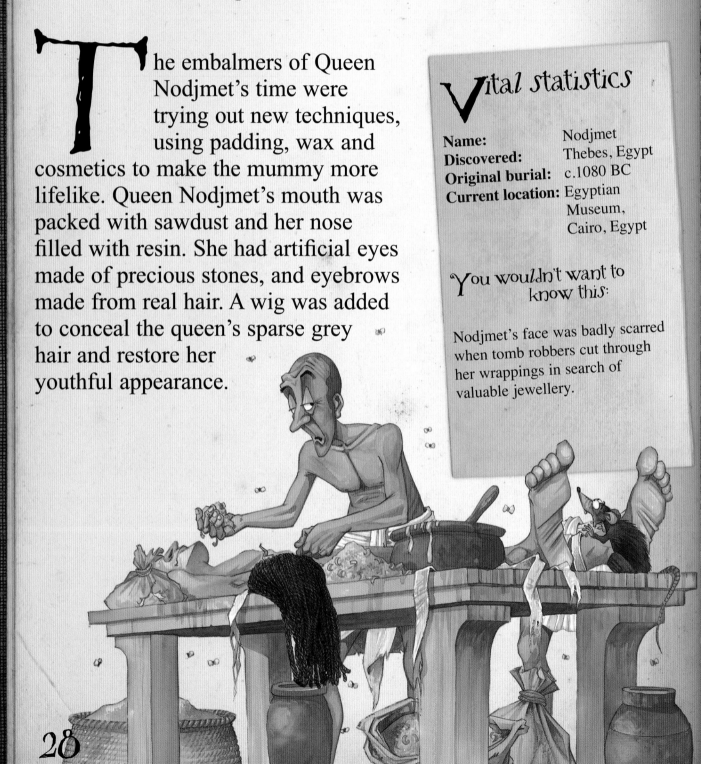

Be prepared!
Always expect the very worst

No way to treat a lady!

As well as the cuts to her forehead, cheeks and nose, Queen Nodjmet's legs were broken and her wrists and collarbone had also been fractured. The priests had to re-wrap the body to conceal the damage.

Hacked!

Queen Nodjmet's mummy was found in a set of coffins that were originally made for a man. They were altered for the queen's use. The coffins were badly damaged by blows from an axe-like tool called an adze.

Empty!

The canopic chest of Queen Nodjmet is guarded by a statue of the jackal-headed god Anubis. But the chest is empty. Why? Because by this time the Egyptians had stopped putting the dead person's organs in canopic jars; now they embalmed the organs and put them back inside the body.

The Big Scream!

Nº 10

Ramesses II

Ramesses II, who was crowned pharaoh in his early twenties, ruled Egypt from about 1279 to 1213 BC. He was originally buried in a tomb of his own in the Valley of the Kings. After the tombs in the Valley were robbed, Ramesses' mummy was re-wrapped by priests and was moved to the tomb of Queen Inhapy for 72 hours. It was then moved again to the tomb of the high priest Pinudjem II.

How do we know this? All this information was detailed in hieroglyphics on the pharaoh's mummy wrappings.

Vital statistics

Name: Ramesses II
Discovered: Valley of the Kings, Egypt
Original burial: 1213 BC
Current location: Egyptian Museum, Cairo, Egypt

You wouldn't want to know this:

It looks as though the embalmers accidentally knocked Ramesses' head off (his neck was very scrawny) and used a piece of wood to join it back on.

Better be quick – he'll be on the move again!

Be prepared!
Always expect the very worst

Well travelled

In 1974 Egyptologists saw that the mummy was deteriorating and decided to send it to Paris for examination and treatment. The mummy was issued with a passport that listed his occupation as 'King – deceased'. Ramesses was met at Le Bourget airport near Paris with full military honours.

Ozymandias

The poem 'Ozymandias', by Percy Shelley, was inspired by a description of a giant statue of Ramesses II. Shelley describes the ruins of the statue standing in the desert, with an inscription that says:

'My name is Ozymandias, king of kings: Look on my works, ye Mighty, and despair!'

The ruined statue reminds us that even the greatest empires cannot last for ever.

Crash!

Looking inside

Since 1895, X-rays have made it possible to examine the insides of mummies without unwrapping them.

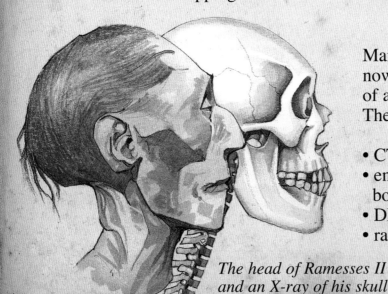

Many new scientific methods are now used to build up our knowledge of ancient Egyptian mummies. These include:

• CT scans (cross-sectional X-rays)
• endoscopy (looking inside the body through a small tube)
• DNA analysis
• radiocarbon dating.

The head of Ramesses II
and an X-ray of his skull

31

The Big Scream!

No 11

Nesyamun

Nesyamun lived around 1100 BC. He was Keeper of the Bulls at the great temple of Amun at Karnak. His mummy was found at Deir el-Bahri near Luxor in 1822. He was sent from Egypt to Trieste in Italy in 1823, then on to London to be exhibited in the Egyptian Hall, Piccadilly. But why was Nesyamun mummified with his tongue sticking out?

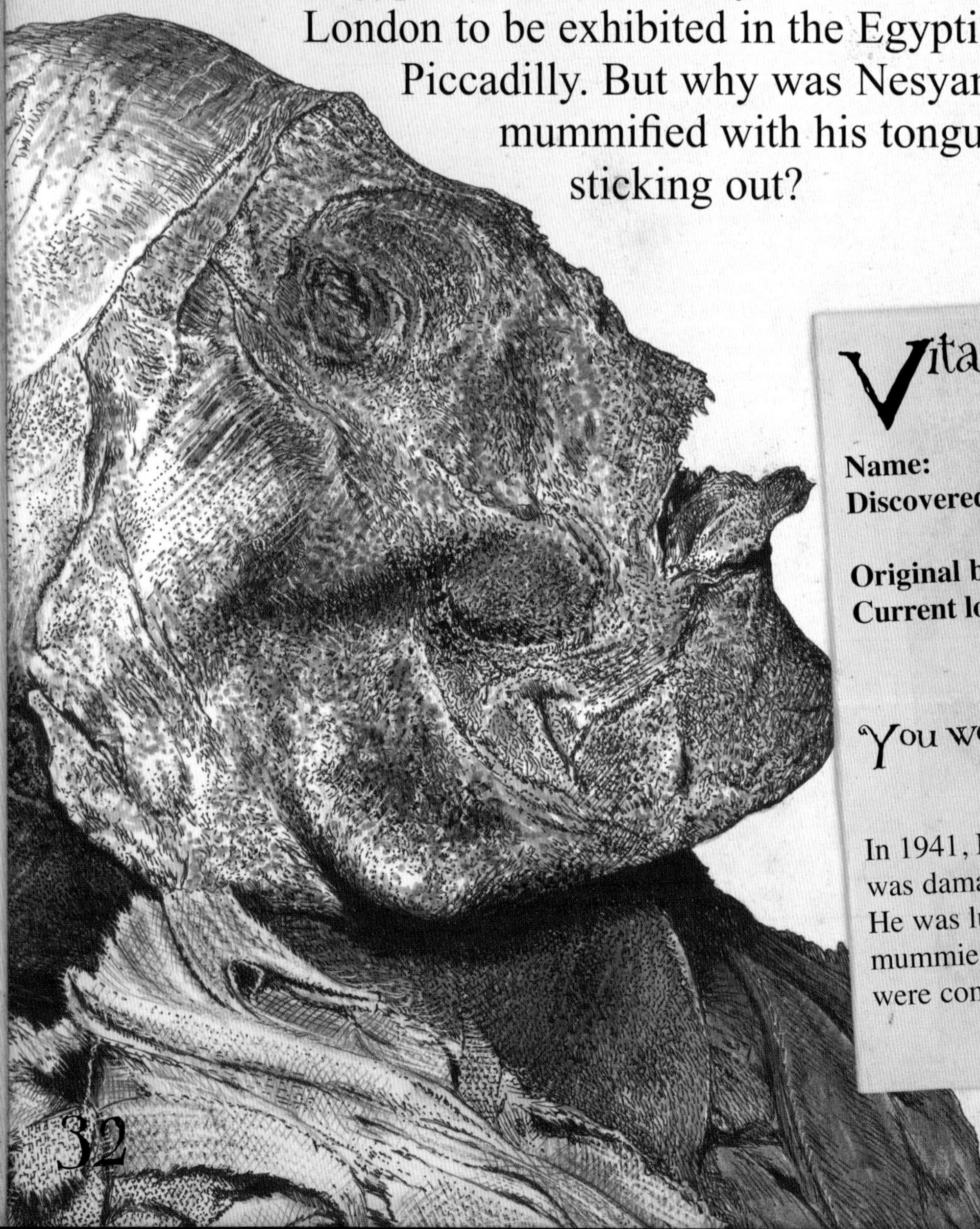

Vital statistics

Name: Nesyamun
Discovered: Deir el-Bahri, Luxor, Egypt
Original burial: c.1100 BC
Current location: City Museum, Leeds, England

You wouldn't want to know this:

In 1941, Nesyamun's mummy was damaged by a wartime bomb. He was lucky: all the other mummies at Leeds Museum were completely destroyed.

Be prepared!
Always expect the very worst

Cause of death

Scientists who examined the body at Leeds in 1828 could not decide how he had died. Was he strangled? Probably not – there are no marks on his neck.

He was examined again in 1989. Did he choke to death after being stung on the tongue by a bee? It's possible.

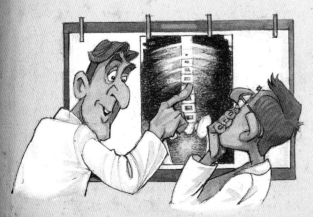

Scientists at Leeds were among the first to use X-rays to study mummies.

A cushy life

We know a lot about Nesyamun's life from the inscriptions on his coffin and the objects buried with him. He was 1.68 m (5 ft 6 in) tall and died in his mid-forties. He was a waab priest, which means that he was allowed to approach the inner sanctum of the great temple of the god Amun. There he performed rituals, recited prayers and made offerings to Amun. But he only had to work for three months of the year – the rest of his time was his own.

A reconstruction of how Nesyamun may have looked when he was alive

33

No 12

Seqenenre Tao II

The mummy of Pharaoh Seqenenre was discovered at Deir el-Bahri in 1881. It was unwrapped in 1886. The detailed report of this examination reveals that the pharaoh died from horrific injuries inflicted by clubs and maces. The pharaoh had survived an earlier head wound which may have left him partly paralysed.

Vital statistics

Name: Seqenenre Tao II
Discovered: Deir el-Bahri, Luxor, Egypt
Original burial: c.1558 BC
Current location: Egyptian Museum, Cairo, Egypt

You wouldn't want to know this:

The embalmers had to do a rush job on the pharaoh's body because it had already begun to rot before they started work.

You won't survive this one!

Be prepared!
Always expect the very worst

French Egyptologist Gaston Maspero unwraps the mummy

From Gaston Maspero's report:

'A blow from an axe must have severed part of his left cheek, exposed the teeth, fractured the jaw, and sent him senseless to the ground.'

Who was he?

Seqenenre Tao II is sometimes referred to as 'the Brave'. He fought against a neighbouring people called the Hyksos, who had been enemies of the Egyptians for centuries. His son Ahmose carried on the fight against the Hyksos, and eventually defeated them.

Was Seqenenre Tao killed in battle against the Hyksos, or was he murdered? We don't know. But, judging by the state of the body, he must have been left where he fell for some time.

Seqenenre Tao II was pharaoh for only a short time, but he did find time to build a mud-brick palace at a place now known as Deir el-Ballas.

'Another blow must have seriously injured the skull, and a dagger or javelin has cut open the forehead on the right side, a little above the eye.'

'The hair is thick, rough and matted; the face had been shaved on the morning of his death.'

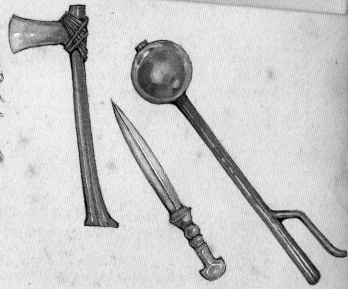

An axe, a dagger and a mace (battle club). Seqenenre Tao was probably killed by weapons like these.

The Big Scream!

No 13

The 'screaming mummy'

In 1886 Gaston Maspero, the head of the Egyptian Antiquities Service, was unwrapping one of the many mummies of kings and queens that had been moved in ancient times to hide them from grave robbers. When this mummy's plain, undecorated coffin was opened, Maspero made a shocking discovery. There, wrapped in a sheep or goat skin, lay the body of a young man, his face screaming in agony, his hands and feet tightly bound.

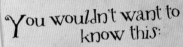

Vital statistics

Name: Prince Pentewere (possibly)

Discovered: Valley of the Kings, Egypt

Original burial: c.1155 BC

Current location: Egyptian Museum, Cairo, Egypt

You wouldn't want to know this:

Sheep and goats were considered unclean by the Egyptians. Wrapping a body in the skin of an unclean animal was a dreadful insult.

Ça alors! (Good Lord!)

Be prepared!
Always expect the very worst

Who was the mystery man?

One theory is that the 'screaming mummy' is Prince Pentewere, son of Pharaoh Ramesses III. Pentewere and his mother, Queen Tiy, were involved in a plot to murder the pharaoh and put Pentewere on the throne.

Ramesses III

Is he really screaming?

Probably not. The gaping jaw may have been caused by the head falling back on the work table as the body was being mummified. Later Egyptian embalmers worked out ways to prevent this from happening.

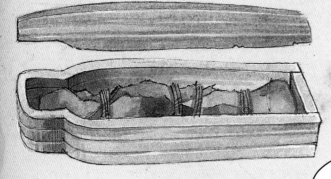

Unnamed for eternity

A papyrus scroll records how the plot was quickly discovered and the plotters were executed. But it seems that Pentewere was not killed along with the others. Because of his royal blood, he was allowed to commit suicide by drinking poison – a less shameful death.

He was buried without a grave marker, so his name would never be known – a punishment that would last for all eternity.

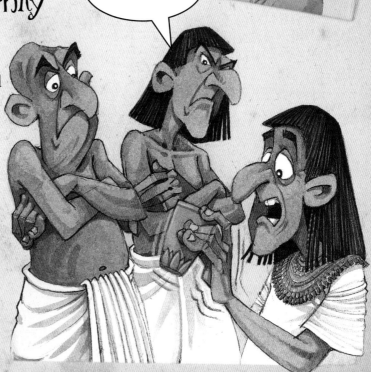

Drink it up!

N₀ 14

Home comforts in Ancient Greece

Originally most Greek people lived and worked in the countryside. But after around 700 BC, towns grew bigger and poor farmers and their servants migrated there. Everywhere, the streets seemed full of people, from proud rich men with bodyguards to beggars in the dirt.

A craftworker's house

Craftworkers in the town lived in houses like this. It would have been one in a block of homes for 10 families. The house is built around a courtyard, containing the family altar where offerings are made to the gods. It is shielded from the street by a strong gate and a high wall.

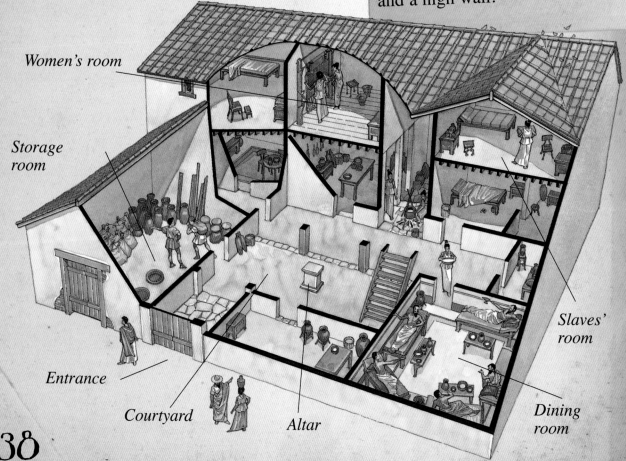

Women's room

Storage room

Entrance

Courtyard

Altar

Slaves' room

Dining room

Be prepared! Always expect the very worst

On the streets

The air was noisy with the hammering, shouting and clatter of horses' hooves. It was also very smelly; there were no sewers. At night, servants with torches escorted groups of partygoers and kept a look out for thieves.

Household chores

Household slaves called 'oiketai' were needed to do the daily tasks. They did all the cooking, cleaning, lighting of fires, and collecting loads of heavy firewood.

Puff!

Living in a town

Towns were also home to slaves and other non-citizens: travelling merchants, craftsmen, scholars and sailors. Overcrowding – and disputes about town government – sometimes led to problems. Athens (population 250,000) faced famine, plague, bitter political rivalry and slave revolts.

Slaves were at the beck and call of their owner's wife. They would be scolded if she wasn't happy with their work.

Stupid slave girl!

Who'd be a slave?

Travel and transport in Greece

The best way to explore a world beyond Greece was to travel by sea – sailing from island to island or along the coast. However, Greek sailors did not like to venture far out of sight of land. They had no compasses to help them steer or fix their positions, and had to rely on the stars. Winter storms made the seas dangerous; many ships were wrecked.

Sea transport

Transport by sea was often quicker than by land. Ships could carry far greater loads than wagons. They brought stone, especially marble, from the Greek islands.

But sea transport had its dangers. Many valuable loads of stone ended up at the bottom of the sea when ships sailed onto rocks or were overcome by storms.

The earliest Greek ships were fairly small (maybe 30 m long) with one bank of oars and a simple sail.

Be prepared!
Always expect the very worst

Bumpy roads

Poor roads with potholes and rough surfaces sometimes caused accidents to happen. Wheels came off wagons and oxen lost their footing and fell!

A   *B*   *C*

D

A guide to travellers

Some people that might have travelled on the bumpy Greek roads could include:

- A: An army porter, carrying food, tools and equipment.

- B: A rich man's groom, driving his master's two-horse cart.

- C: A young traveller, riding a fast, well-bred horse.

- D: An army officer and driver, in a four-horse war chariot.

Journeys by road

Narrow mountain passes were for walkers or sure-footed mules. Better paths ran along the coast in eastern Greece where the mountains sloped gently down to the sea. They were built for wheeled traffic: fast chariots or lumbering farm carts stacked with huge clay jars of grain.

In 490 BC, during the Persian wars, a messenger ran all the way – 42 km – from the plains of Marathon to Athens to announce an Athenian victory.

The first marathon

Huff! Puff!

№16

The Olympic Games

The Olympic Games were very important to the ancient Greeks. So important that even wars were halted to let the sports festival take place. However, the events needed a lot of training and were often so dangerous that they resulted in serious injury. And that's not to mention the foul play!

Watch out!

Though the competition was a religious event, not all the spectators were honourable. The large crowds attracted all sorts of undesirable characters.

Pancratium

Just about anything goes in this event. It was a mixture of boxing and wrestling. Competitors were allowed to choke and punch each other, even when they were on the floor. Fighters were known to have died from their injuries. However, it was forbidden to kill opponents in the wrestling or boxing matches, either deliberately or accidentally.

Thump!

Be prepared!
Always expect the very worst

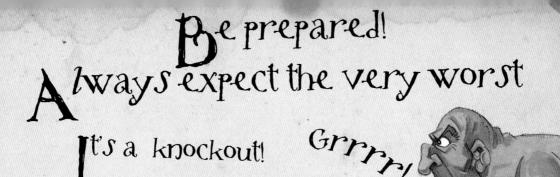

It's a knockout!

Grrrr!

Boxers were terrifying to look at. They wore leather padding on their hands; some had metal studs to inflict extra pain on their opponents. There was no allowance made for differences in opponents' size.

Eeek!

Obeying the rules

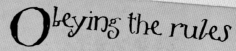

Every contest was watched closely by referees to make sure that no-one was cheating. Athletes who cheated could be disqualified, or they might have to pay a fine to the Olympic committee. The worst crime of all was bribing a referee or an opponent.

On horseback

Chariot races were seen as good practice for war. Up to 40 chariots took part in a single race, so the sport was very dangerous. At the turning posts, the chariots often got tangled up. Collisions were common and accidents and injuries ranged from minor sprains to broken bones and even death.

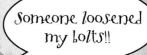

Someone loosened my bolts!!

43

No 17

Sickness and health in Ancient Rome

Doctors were available for ancient Romans, but they were expensive so many people opted for a local chemist or spent the night in the temple of Aesculapius, the god of healing. Doctors usually treated illnesses with herbal medicines, such as a mustard gargle for a stomach ulcer. They also carried out operations using wine as an anaesthetic!

Battle wounds

Army doctors were highly respected and were assisted by dressers, who treated wounds during battles and nursed the soldiers back to health. Common battle wounds included jagged sword cuts, broken bones and dislocated joints. Sometimes damaged limbs had to be amputated. Salt, arsenic and turpentine were used as antiseptics and kept wounds from becoming infected.

Relax – this won't hurt ... well not much, anyway.

Oww!

Be prepared!
Always expect the very worst

Bewitching illnesses

Despite their advanced technology, Romans believed that illness could be caused by witchcraft. To find a cure, they gave presents to the witch, begging her to remove the spell, or made a special visit to a temple to ask the gods to make them better.

A hospital in a Roman fort.

Injured soldiers bandaged their wounds with cobwebs soaked in vinegar. This helped the soldiers but wasn't so good for the spiders!

Demon barbers

Going to the barber's could be very painful. Barbers used shears to trim men's hair and beards. When a smooth, close-shaven look was in fashion, barbers had to pull men's beards out by the roots, one hair at a time!

Cured by cabbage?

Cabbage was one of the most popular plant remedies. It was crushed and spread on bruises and boils; stewed for headaches; fried in hot fat to treat sleeplessness; dried, powdered and sniffed to clear blocked noses; and squeezed to extract juice to use as ear drops!*

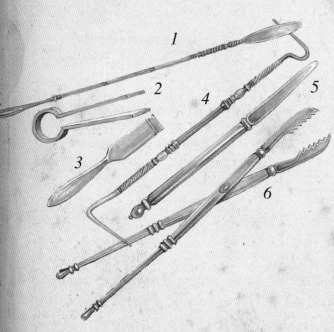

1. Spatula (knife for spreading ointment)
2. Tweezers
3. Probe used for shallow wounds
4. Hook
5. Knife used for surgery
6. Forceps

*The Salariya Book Company takes NO responsibility for the advice given on this page.

The Big Scream!

Life in the army in Rome

A soldier's life was brutal. They might die in battle or from diseases caught on campaign. Even when they were not fighting, they spent long hours training or building roads and forts. Their food was simple and their discipline harsh. Each legion had about 5,000 soldiers, divided into smaller units of 80 men, called centuries.

Grrr!

Army discipline

Army discipline was ferocious. Men who ran away or disobeyed orders were killed. One commander even executed his own son. Savage punishments like 'decimation' forced soldiers to behave. If just one man in a cohort (unit of 500 soldiers) broke the rules, one in every ten was killed, even though most of them had done nothing wrong!

The Romans liked to collect their enemies' heads as trophies.

Now I'm in the army, I may never see my homeland again!

46

Be prepared!
Always expect the very worst

Left!   Right!   Left!   Right!

Left, right, left, right!

Marching made the legionaries strong and fit. They had to cover distances of 20 miles (32 km) at a quick pace in five hours. The soldiers were nicknamed 'Marius's mules', after a famous general, because they had to march with all their equipment on their backs.

Sandals had heavy studs on the soles to prevent the leather from wearing down quickly.

Great load

Each soldier had to march carrying his armour, weapons, helmet, shield, cloak, leather bottle (for water or wine), cooking pot, metal dish, spade and mattock (for digging defensive ditches), first-aid kit and two weeks' food. All this weighed over 40 kg!

Hmph! This week my duties include cleaning all the centurions' boots!

I'm cleaning the latrines all week!

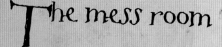

The mess room

Eight men were supposed to share each pair of mess rooms. The rooms were cramped and gloomy places to live. One room was used for sleeping, and the other was for storing, cleaning and repairing equipment. All the soldiers had to cook, eat and relax there together.

Roman religion and superstition

The ancient Romans believed in many different gods and goddesses. These were split into two groups. Roman homes were protected by household gods – the lares and the penates. The gods in the second group were those of the official state religion. People feared these gods and tried to keep them happy with offerings and sacrifices. If things went wrong, they believed it was because the gods were angry.

Eastern cults

Some Roman soldiers found the state religion too stuffy and impersonal and turned instead to cults from the east. Some promised their followers life after death. They were regarded with suspicion by officers because they encouraged non-Roman behaviour, lessening their loyalty to Rome and its emperors.

Mars

Venus

Jupiter is the king of the gods and Juno his wife. His daughter Venus is the goddess of love and his son Mars is the god of war.

Juno

Jupiter

Be prepared!
Always expect the very worst

Symbols of good and evil

- Balding men may stop their hair falling out by sniffing cyclamen flowers!

- The sound of bells is thought to ease a woman's pain in childbirth.

- Bees are sacred messengers of the gods and symbols of good luck.

- Peony flowers have special, magical powers of healing the sick and ill.

- Eagles, emblems of the Roman legions, are said to bring thunderstorms.

Cursed enemies!

Romans often asked the gods to curse their enemies. They wrote their enemies' names, plus curse words, on scraps of metal or pottery and left them at temples. They hoped that the gods would see these messages, and harm the people named in them.

Christianity banned!

Some of the world's first Christians lived in Rome. But until AD 313 Christianity was banned in the Roman Empire. Christians met secretly, in underground passages called catacombs, to say prayers and hold services. They also used the catacombs as a burial place.

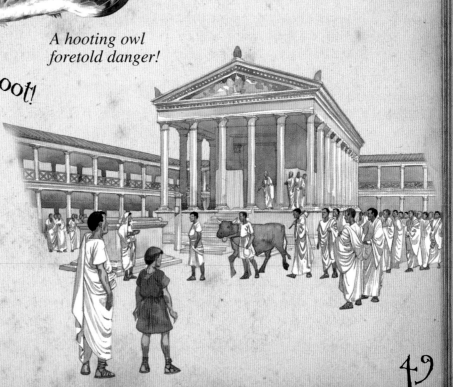

A hooting owl foretold danger!

Hooot!

After an animal had been sacrificed to the gods, a priest, called a haruspex, examined its liver. If it was diseased, bad luck was on the way!

49

The Big Scream!

Life and death in Pompeii

Pompeii was a bustling town not far from Rome, in the south of Italy. In the year AD 79, a nearby volcano erupted, and buried the town in ash. Pompeii lay hidden for centuries until, one day, some farmers discovered its Roman remains...

Warning signs

In AD 62 an earthquake rocked Pompeii and the countryside around. As the ground shook, statues and buildings wobbled until they cracked and fell. This was a warning sign from Mount Vesuvius. By AD 79, life had returned to normal for the people of Pompeii, until they started to notice lots of odd things...

Strong shakes were felt; cups and plates got broken.

Loud booming noises came from under the ground.

Wells and springs dried up.

The River Sarno was full of dead fish.

Smoke and gas started coming out of holes in the ground.

Grapes withered on the vines.

Hmm?

Be prepared!
Always expect the very worst

Aaah!

Panic in Pompeii!

- The people of Pompeii gathered up their belongings and tried to leave town.

- Some people seized the chance to steal from the empty houses.

- From late afternoon roofs caved in under the weight of the pumice.

- Pumice floats, and it soon clogged up the River Sarno.

- The choking smell of rotten eggs in the air increased and it became harder to breathe.

Death of a town

In AD 79 millions of tonnes of red-hot volcanic debris surged down the mountain at great speed, quickly reaching the town wall. It was all over in just 30 minutes. Pompeii, the town that 15,000 people had called home, was buried beneath a deep layer of ash.

Pompeii uncovered

The modern story of Pompeii begins in 1748, when treasure-hunters began the first of many excavations to find valuable objects. Today, Pompeii is a Roman time capsule, and as visitors walk along the ancient streets and look into shops and houses, it's as if they have been transported back in time to AD 79.

In the 1860s, Giuseppe Fiorelli poured plaster into hollowed areas in the ash where bodies had lain.

Lost in AD 79 …

…and found almost 2,000 years later!

51

52

Petrifying People

G hastly gangsters, vicious Vikings and putrid pirates. You wouldn't want to meet anyone in this rogues' gallery!

№o 21

Erik Bloodaxe

Erik Bloodaxe! His name says it all. Even for violent Vikings, Erik was a bit too bloodthirsty. Born in Norway, he became a Viking pirate at just 12 years old. Then he killed four of his own brothers to make sure that he became king. But Erik was a cruel and unjust ruler, so the Norwegians (plus a brave surviving sixth brother) drove him out.

Vital statistics

Name: Erik Haraldsson
Nickname: Bloodaxe
Born: Norway
Ruled: Norway c.AD 931–933; Jorvik c.947–948 and 952–954
Career: Pirate, king
Dreadful deeds: Killing and raiding
Died: Killed at Stainmore, near Durham, England

You wouldn't want to know this:

Erik's wife Gunnild was trained as a witch. People said she could fly, and she certainly could concoct some very nasty poisons. She was eventually punished by being drowned in a bog.

They don't call me Bloodaxe for nothing!

Be prepared!
Always expect the very worst

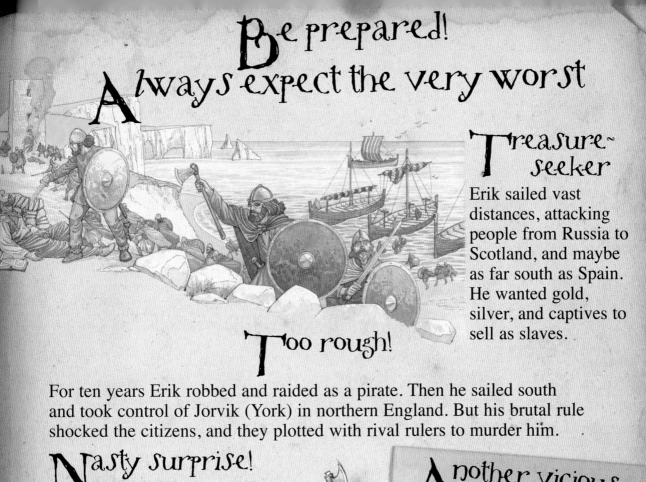

Treasure-seeker

Erik sailed vast distances, attacking people from Russia to Scotland, and maybe as far south as Spain. He wanted gold, silver, and captives to sell as slaves.

Too rough!

For ten years Erik robbed and raided as a pirate. Then he sailed south and took control of Jorvik (York) in northern England. But his brutal rule shocked the citizens, and they plotted with rival rulers to murder him.

Nasty surprise!

Driven out of Jorvik, Erik was attacked and killed by Scottish warriors. Was it a planned ambush? Yes, probably!

Another vicious Viking

The Normans were Viking raiders who settled in France. In 1066 they invaded England, led by Duke William (later known as 'the Conqueror'). When the northern English rebelled, William set fire to their houses and crops, and destroyed their goods, tools and weapons. Countless families starved to death, and the land did not recover for 100 years.

Tremble!

Henry VIII

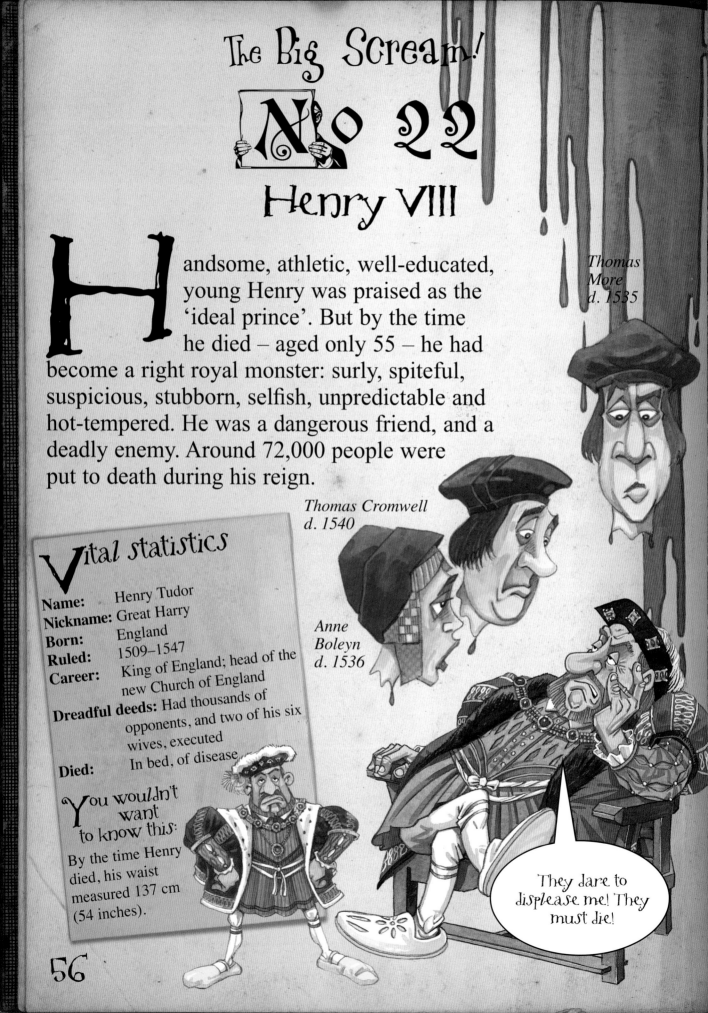

Handsome, athletic, well-educated, young Henry was praised as the 'ideal prince'. But by the time he died – aged only 55 – he had become a right royal monster: surly, spiteful, suspicious, stubborn, selfish, unpredictable and hot-tempered. He was a dangerous friend, and a deadly enemy. Around 72,000 people were put to death during his reign.

*Thomas More
d. 1535*

*Thomas Cromwell
d. 1540*

*Anne
Boleyn
d. 1536*

Vital statistics

Name: Henry Tudor
Nickname: Great Harry
Born: England
Ruled: 1509–1547
Career: King of England; head of the new Church of England
Dreadful deeds: Had thousands of opponents, and two of his six wives, executed
Died: In bed, of disease

You wouldn't want to know this:
By the time Henry died, his waist measured 137 cm (54 inches).

They dare to displease me! They must die!

Be prepared!
Always expect the very worst

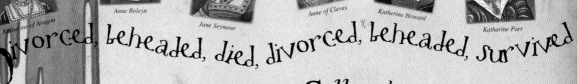

Katharine of Aragon — Anne Boleyn — Jane Seymour — Anne of Cleves — Katherine Howard — Katharine Parr

Divorced, beheaded, died, divorced, beheaded, survived

The search for a son

Henry needed a male heir to rule after him. So he married again and again – but only his last, childless, marriage was happy.

Katherine Howard d. 1542

Edward Stafford d. 1521

Cardinal Thomas Wolsey d. 1530

Fallen hero

In 1536 Henry fell from his horse during a joust (mock battle). The blow on the head made him depressed and bad-tempered for the rest of his life.

Nnngh

Bloody Mary

Henry VIII's oldest daughter, Mary I (ruled 1553–1558), was every bit as determined as her father. But, unlike him, she did not want the Church in England to be independent from the Roman Catholic Church. She executed over 300 Protestant men and women who did not share her Catholic beliefs.

Off with their heads!

King Henry was ruthless about getting his own way. His wives and advisors stayed safe only while they pleased him. Disobedience might mean death!

No 23

Cleopatra

Beautiful but deadly – and maybe misunderstood – Cleopatra was the last queen to rule ancient Egypt. She lost a mighty kingdom, saw her people starve – and had love-affairs with two enemy Roman generals. Did she neglect her country to follow the men she loved? Or did she use her beauty and charm to try to stop the Romans invading? If she did, she failed. After 3,000 glorious years, proud, rich Egypt was conquered by Rome in 30 BC.

Vital statistics

Name: Cleopatra VII Philopator
Nicknames: Great Lady of Perfection, Queen of Kings
Born: Egypt
Ruled: 51–30 BC
Career: Queen of Egypt
Dreadful deeds: Arranging family murders
Died: Suicide, by snakebite or poison

You wouldn't want to know this:

Cleopatra spent a fortune on clothes and feasts, while many Egyptians were poor and hungry.

Hidden charms

In 48 BC, Roman commander Julius Caesar arrived in Egypt. Cleopatra was afraid that her brother would kill her so that he could rule alone. So she smuggled herself into Caesar's room to ask for his protection.

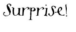

Surprise!

Bewitching!

Be prepared!
Always expect the very worst

family matters

Caesar and
Cleopatra fell
in love – and
Cleopatra's
brother was found
dead. Suspicious
deaths happened
all too often in

Cleopatra's family: both her brothers and
all three of her sisters died before her,
either executed or murdered.

You look divine, dear

Caesar paid for a gold
statue of Cleopatra looking
like Isis, the Egyptian
goddess of life and love.
Roman priests and
people were shocked.

Bearded lady

Not everyone approved of
female rulers. To show that
she was just as good as a man,
Egyptian Queen Hatshepsut
(ruled 1508–1458 BC) wore a
false beard, a traditional sign
of kingly power.

Who, me?*

Death – and dishonour

Caesar helped Cleopatra
stay in power. But he
was murdered in 44 BC. Now who would
protect her? In 41 BC Cleopatra fell in love
with a second Roman leader, Mark Antony.
Together they planned to rule Egypt and
conquer a vast empire, free from Roman
control. But their army was defeated in
31 BC. In disgrace and despair, they
killed themselves.

*Some say that Cleopatra committed suicide
by teasing a poisonous snake until it bit her.

No 24

King John

The only king of England to be nicknamed 'bad', John was short, stout, richly dressed and very fond of women – and luxuries. John passed harsh new laws, grabbed land and treasures, mocked the Church, and did nothing to help poor, ordinary people. Worst of all, his disastrous wars lost rich English lands in France – and he threatened the ancient legal rights of his subjects.

Vital statistics

Name: John Plantagenet
Nicknames: Lackland, Softsword
Born: England
Ruled: 1199–1216
Career: Lord of Ireland, Prince in Aquitaine (western France), King of England
Dreadful deeds: Greedy and unjust; his wars lost half a kingdom
Died: Of dysentery

You wouldn't want to know this:
When John lost his temper he would gnaw his fingers in fury.

Lost in the Wash

In 1216 King John was taken ill while travelling. He went back to bed (where, in 6 days, he died). But he sent his horses, laden with favourite royal jewels, by a short cut over a marshy bay known as the Wash. Trapped by the tide, the horses drowned, and the jewels were lost.

Be prepared!
Always expect the very worst

Magna Carta

John's harsh rule made the barons (nobles) angry. In 1215 they drew up a Great Charter – a list of their demands. The most important: no imprisonment without trial, and no new taxes unless the barons were consulted.

I'll sign it, but I won't stick to it.

That'll teach him!

Birth of a legend?

Stories about outlaw hero Robin Hood may have started after King John gave new powers to royal officials such as sheriffs. Poor people complained that John's officials were cruel, greedy and unjust – and the Sheriff of Nottingham became Robin's great enemy.

Expensive tastes

King John needed cash – to pay for his wars, his castles, his jewels, his fine clothes and his girlfriends. He also gave expensive gifts to his friends, to make sure they kept on supporting him. How did he get the money? By raising taxes, and sending fierce tax collectors all round his kingdom.

Hand it over!

You're banned!

John wanted to name his own Church officials, but the Pope insisted this was his duty. To punish John, the Pope placed England under an Interdict (religious ban), which meant that no-one could marry or hold a funeral. Ordinary people were very upset – and furious with John.

The Big Scream!

No 25

Maximilien Robespierre

'The King must die!' shouted angry mobs in the streets of Paris, France. In 1789 they launched a revolution to get rid of King Louis XVI and win power for themselves. From 1793 to 1794, Robespierre was their leader. Around 40,000 'enemies of the state' – including most of the royal family – were killed during his bloody Reign of Terror.

Guillotine

Vital statistics

Name: Maximilien François Marie Isidore de Robespierre

Nickname: The Incorruptible*

Born: France

Lived: 1758–1794

Career: Lawyer, then revolutionary

Dreadful deeds: Led bloodthirsty Reign of Terror

Died: Executed by guillotine

You wouldn't want to know this:

He tried to kill himself the night before his execution. He was probably scared by stories of victims' heads that went on living and feeling pain after they had been cut off.

*Incorruptible: always honest.

Be prepared!
Always expect the very worst

Word power

Robespierre won support for the French Revolution by making rousing speeches, and by his pure and honest lifestyle. But his ideas became dangerously extreme. He thought terror and bloodshed were the only way to run the new revolutionary government. After a year as leader, he was condemned to die.

What about the workers?

The revolution of 1789 began with protests by poor, starving workers. Their lives were hard and they paid heavy taxes, while French royalty – especially pretty, silly Queen Marie Antoinette – led lives of luxury. They had to go!

> They have no bread? Let them eat cake!

> Liberty, equality, fraternity – or death!

Out of control

During Robespierre's Reign of Terror, thousands of Paris citizens were guillotined. But thousands more nobles, priests, government officials and ordinary people were killed by angry mobs in the countryside. Robespierre could not stop the mass slaughter he had started. The revolution was out of control!

63

Nᵒ 26

The first Chinese emperor

Qin Shi Huangdi was the first man to unite the warring states of China and create one huge Chinese empire. The Great Wall he ordered to defend his country is one of the Wonders of the World. So is his secret tomb, guarded by the famous Terracotta Warriors. But countless millions died working on his massive building schemes.

Vital statistics

Name: Prince Ying Zheng
Title: Qin Shi Huangdi*
Born: Kingdom of Qin
Ruled: Qin, 246–221 BC; all of China, 221–210 BC
Career: First ruler of all China
Dreadful deeds: Executed many enemies; millions died working for him
Died: From taking mercury pills, which he hoped would make him live for ever

You wouldn't want to know this:

Afraid of dying, he sent explorers to search for the magic Elixir of Life. They never found it, of course, but dared not return to tell him.

*First All-Powerful Chinese Emperor

> They call this Wall the biggest tomb in the world – so work until you die!

Be prepared!
Always expect the very worst

Last empress

Ambitious, determined – and beautiful – Cixi was the very last empress of China. She ruled on behalf of her young son Tongzhi (1861–1874) and then for his cousin Guangxu (1875–1908). Some call her corrupt and greedy. Others say that she did her best to protect the ancient Chinese empire during very difficult times.

Burning books

Qin Shi Huangdi wanted to keep firm control of his new empire. So he ordered fine new coins, weights and measures, new roads, canals, ships and wagons, and a new way of writing. He outlawed writers and thinkers, burned books he disagreed with, and buried scholars alive.

I demand immortality!

Death mission

When Qin Shi Huangdi died, his courtiers were afraid to tell anyone. So they carried his decaying body for many miles to his tomb, followed by a cartload of rotting fish to disguise the smell. Once the emperor was safely buried, nearly all the tomb workers were killed, so that they would not reveal the secrets of the tomb.

Fish cart

Nο 27

Ivan the Terrible

Vital statistics

Name: Ivan IV Vasilyevich
Nickname: Grozniy (Terrible or Awesome)
Born: Moscow, Russia
Ruled: 1533–1584
Career: First tsar of Russia
Dreadful deeds: Massacred his own subjects
Died: Possibly murdered

You wouldn't want to know this:

It was rumoured that Ivan's secret police carried real dead dogs' heads to terrify their enemies.

A t first, Ivan IV's reign was glorious. He reformed the government and the law, paid for wonderful new buildings, encouraged art, craft and trade, and conquered Siberia. But as Ivan grew older, his behaviour changed. Was he ill? Or mad? Being slowly poisoned? Or just wicked?

Ivan quarrelled with the people of Novgorod. He declared that he was the punishing 'Hand of God', and gave orders for them all to be killed. Around 60,000 died.

Be prepared!
Always expect the very worst

Cruel reward

Tsar Ivan paid for the best architect in Russia to design an amazing new cathedral for Moscow. According to legend, when the building work was done, Ivan had the architect blinded so that he could never build anything better.

Unfair, unfree

Ivan took away the freedom of the Russian peasants (farm workers). They became serfs – almost slaves. Farmers actually owned them, like animals.

The Tsar's Dogs

Ivan created a new and terrible secret police force, the *Oprichniki*. Nicknamed 'the Tsar's Dogs'', they spied on the Russian people and were free to murder, burn, loot and destroy.

St Basil's Cathedral

Nobody expects the *Oprichniki.*

Death comes home

Ivan brutally beat his son's wife, because he thought her clothes were immodest. Ivan's son tried to defend her – but his father's big stick hit him on the head. Ivan's son died, and his wife lost the baby she was expecting – a double tragedy.

67

№ 25

Vlad Țepeș

IF, IF, IF all the reports about Prince Vlad are true, he must have been one of the most wicked rulers ever. But many of the worst tales were told by his enemies, who may have exaggerated them. We do know, however, that Vlad fought bravely to defend his homeland against invaders – and killed his enemies in a very cruel and revolting way.

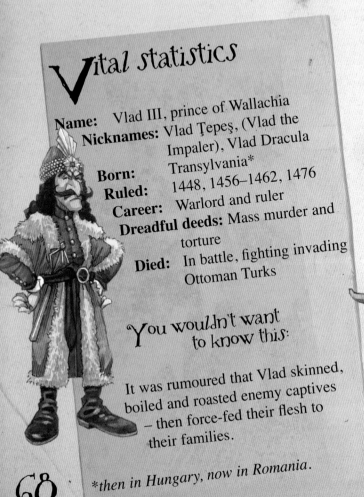

Vital statistics

Name: Vlad III, prince of Wallachia
Nicknames: Vlad Țepeș, (Vlad the Impaler), Vlad Dracula
Born: Transylvania*
Ruled: 1448, 1456–1462, 1476
Career: Warlord and ruler
Dreadful deeds: Mass murder and torture
Died: In battle, fighting invading Ottoman Turks

You wouldn't want to know this:

It was rumoured that Vlad skinned, boiled and roasted enemy captives – then force-fed their flesh to their families.

*then in Hungary, now in Romania.

Hero and monster – that's me!

Be prepared! Always expect the very worst

Vampire name, vampire nature?

Dracula – Dragon's Son – that's what they called Vlad. His father's nickname had been 'Dragon' – and Vlad was just as dangerous! Many years later, in 1896, Irish novelist Bram Stoker used Dracula as the name for his bloodthirsty vampire villain. It became famous worldwide.

But was the real Vlad a vampire? No!

A terrible warning

Vlad's favourite way of killing people was by impaling – hammering huge wooden stakes through them. Why was he so cruel? Because he wanted to bring law and order to his homeland, and keep enemies away. He hoped that his brutal executions would terrify criminals and invaders.

Vlad also killed to end the power of ancient noble familes; he feared they might rebel against him. So he forced top noblemen to build his new castle. They had to work – naked – until they collapsed and died.

Vlad spent years fighting Turkish invaders. He even attacked peaceful messengers sent by Turkey to his court. Grimly, he joked that they'd been slow to show him respect by removing their turbans. So he murdered them by nailing the hats to their heads.

It's war!

No 29

Leopold II

In the 19th century, powerful European nations grew rich from trading with their overseas colonies. Belgium had no colonies, but King Leopold II wanted an empire of his own. In 1885 he paid soldiers and explorers to take control of the Congo region* in Africa. He made a fortune from trade – but treated African people with appalling cruelty.

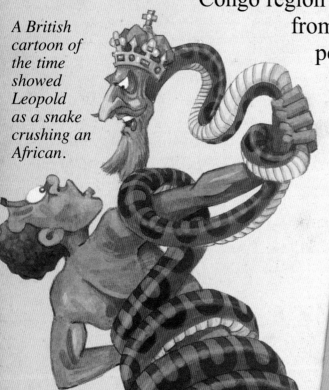

A British cartoon of the time showed Leopold as a snake crushing an African.

Vital statistics

Name: Léopold Louis Philippe Marie Victor; Leopold II of Belgium
Born: Belgium
Ruled: 1865–1909
Career: King of Belgium
Dreadful deeds: Killing and exploiting African people; denying their human rights
Died: Of old age, safely at home in Belgium

You wouldn't want to know this:

By the end of his life, Leopold was so unpopular that his funeral procession was booed.

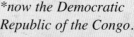

now the Democratic Republic of the Congo.

Be prepared!
Always expect the very worst

Savage slavery

The Congo Free State (as it was called) belonged to Leopold himself, not to Belgium. If Leopold's African slave-workers did not supply enough ivory or rubber, he had their hands cut off. Others were beaten so badly that they died. Probably half the people in the Congo Free State were killed, or died of hunger and sickness, during Leopold's reign.

Something must be done

In 1904, missionaries set up the Congo Reform Association to tell the world about the shocking abuses there. The British government ordered a report on the subject. The news of Leopold's cruelty caused international outrage, and in 1908 the Belgian government took over control of the Congo. It became an independent country in 1960.

A delicate matter

King Leopold was a close relative of Britain's Queen Victoria. So, while she lived, the British government found it difficult to criticise his terrible crimes. But as soon as Victoria died, in 1901, British politicians felt free to speak out.

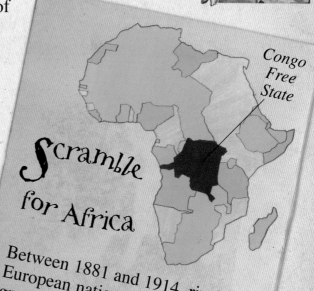

Congo Free State

Scramble for Africa

Between 1881 and 1914, rival European nations competed greedily to grab vast areas of land in Africa. They wanted Africa's rich resources: gold, diamonds, copper, rubber and ivory.

No 30

Nero

Too much, too young! Nero became Roman emperor – the mightiest ruler in the western world – when he was only 17. The power quickly went to his head. Desperate to win popularity with the Roman people, he ignored wise advice, spent government money wildly and provoked rebellion against his rule. Worst of all, he seems positively to have enjoyed killing anyone who displeased him.

Vital statistics

Birth name: Lucius Domitius Ahenobarbus
Name as emperor: Nero Claudius Caesar Augustus Germanicus
Born: Rome, Italy
Ruled: AD 54–69
Career: Roman emperor
Dreadful deeds: Murdered his family and political rivals, persecuted Christians
Died: Killed himself to escape assassination

You wouldn't want to know this: Nero may have started a massive fire that wrecked half of Rome, just to clear space for his new palace.

They say I played music while Rome burned – not true!

Be prepared!
Always expect the very worst

Horrid husband

Nero divorced his first wife, exiled her from Rome, then had her executed when she returned. When Nero's second wife suddenly collapsed and died, people said that he had kicked her to death.

Bloodstained dynasty

In AD 54 Nero's mother, Agrippina, killed Nero's stepfather, Emperor Claudius, so that Nero could seize power. The next year, Nero poisoned his teenage stepbrother Britannicus, who had a better right to rule. Then, in AD 59, Nero killed his own mother. He suspected she was plotting against him.

No contest

No-one criticised Nero and survived! He killed countless people who complained about his policies. He forced everyone to applaud when he sang in public. He insisted on competing in chariot races at the Olympic Games, and made sure the judges declared him the winner.

Tra-la!

Thrown to the lions

Nero thought Christians were a threat to Roman power. So he had them killed in extremely nasty ways – by burning them alive, crucifying them, feeding them to ravenous dogs, using them as bait for wild beasts in the arena, or making them fight trained gladiators.

Tipu Sultan

Famed for his fierceness – and for wearing clothes striped like a tiger – Tipu Sultan fought to defend India, his homeland, from invaders. He failed (his kingdom was conquered by British armies in 1799), but won worldwide respect for his courage. 'Better to live one day as a tiger than a lifetime as a sheep!' he said.

Vital Statistics

Name: Sultan Fateh Ali Khan Shahab

Nickname: Tipu Sultan/The Tiger of Mysore

Born: India

Lived: 1750 to 1799

Career: Warrior and ruler

Fought: British troops in India, and rival Indian rulers

Died: Defending his capital city

You wouldn't want to know this:

Tipu threw prisoners into tiger pits to be killed, or so his enemies said.

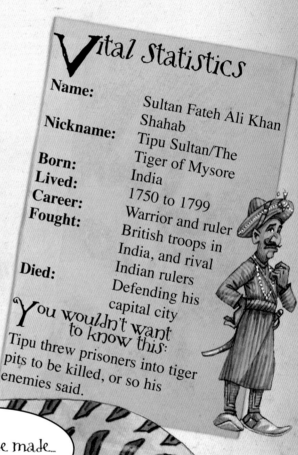

Life-size musical model of a tiger devouring a British soldier.

Tipu had me made...

...to frighten Europeans! Owww!

Be prepared!
Always expect the very worst
fierce as a tiger

How did Tipu win his nickname? By killing a huge tiger. It sprang at him when his gun failed to fire, but Tipu fought back, armed only with a dagger.

Dinner!

Rowr!

Soldier Queen

Nature knows best

Tipu was not the only Indian warrior to fight like a tiger. War-leader Shivaji (lived 1630 to 1680) killed his enemies using fearsome metal blades fixed to his fingers.

Rani Lakshmibai (lived 1835 to 1858) learned horse-riding, archery and self-defence. She used these skills to fight the British. She died fighting bravely alongside her men.

Swoosh

I call them my tiger-claws!

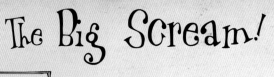

No 32

Boudicca

When Boudicca's husband died, he left half his kingdom to the Romans. But they demanded it all, and attacked Boudicca's family. Outraged, she led Celtic tribes to smash and burn Roman cities, sparing no-one. The Romans said her troops loved to 'glut themselves on the blood of their enemies'.

Vital Statistics

Name:	Boudicca
Nickname:	Not known, but 'Boudicca' means 'Victory'
Born:	Eastern England
Lived:	Birth date unknown – died AD 61
Career:	King's wife, then (after he died) ruling queen
Fought:	Roman conquerors
Died:	Killed herself to avoid capture

You wouldn't want to know this:

Boudicca had knives fixed to her chariot's wheels, to slice up enemy soldiers.

Look out, London, here we come!

Slice

Be prepared!
Always expect the very worst

The final battle

Boudicca's brave but reckless Celtic troops were no match for trained Roman soldiers. In AD 61, in Middle England, around 80,000 Celts were stabbed to death by Roman spears. Only 400 Romans died.

No surrender!

As Roman soldiers surrounded her chariot, Boudicca took poison and died. Her rebellion had failed, and she was too proud – and too angry – to let the Romans capture her alive.

Another royal rebel

Far away, in Palmyra (now Syria), another proud queen fought for independence. Zenobia (lived AD 240 to 274) kicked out Roman governors and invaded Egypt, before the Romans captured her. She died in prison, probably beheaded.

Hernando Cortés

Young, noble, but poor, Cortés was eager for adventure – and gold. In 1518 he set out to conquer the Aztec empire in Mexico – using trickery and savage punishments, such as burning captives alive. Other *conquistadors* followed him, and by 1600 most of South America was ruled by Spain.

Vital Statistics

Name:	Hernando (or Hernán) Cortés
Nickname:	'Conquistador' (Conqueror)
Born:	Spain
Lived:	1485 to 1547
Career:	Soldier, explorer
Fought:	Aztecs and pirates
Died:	Of disease, back home in Spain

You wouldn't want to know this:

When Cortés landed in Mexico, he burned the ships he had arrived in. He was determined to conquer – or die trying!

Cortés tortured their emperor, and now the Aztecs are fighting back!

It's a Noche Triste (Sad Night). But we'll be back – and we'll crucify them!*

*This is how Cortés punished Aztecs who resisted him.

Be prepared!
Always expect the very worst

Holy stone

This magnificent carved stone shows a powerful Aztec prophecy: the world would end when the god Quetzalcoatl arrived from over the sea. For a while, Aztecs suspected that Cortés might be the god, and because horses were unknown in Mexico, they feared that his soldiers on horseback might be magical monsters.

Deadly diseases

The diseases spread by the conquerors, such as measles and smallpox, were even more deadly than their weapons. By around 1600, about 5 out of every 6 Aztecs had died.

Gah!

Lautaro

One Native American hero almost defeated the conquistadors. From 1553 until 1557, Lautaro led the Mapuche people of Chile to fight the Spanish invaders. They had very nearly won when Lautaro was betrayed and killed.

At first the Aztecs welcomed Cortés. But he captured Aztec emperor Moctezuma, and brutally executed Aztec generals. The Aztecs fought back bravely, but their traditional weapons were powerless against European guns. By 1521 Cortés had conquered them.

Nʘ 34

Julius Caesar

Brave, ruthless, and very, very clever, Caesar was one of ancient Rome's greatest army commanders. He conquered rich nations, reformed the government, wowed crowds with his speeches and even changed the way time was measured (we still use his calendar today). But Caesar was also frighteningly ambitious. When he took total control of Rome his enemies killed him to set the Roman people free.

Vital Statistics

Name: Gaius Julius Caesar

Nickname: The name Caesar was used as a royal title for 2,000 years.

Born: Rome, Italy

Lived: 100 BC – 44 BC

Career: Soldier and politician

Fought: To win land for Rome, and power for himself

Died: Stabbed (23 times!) by political enemies.

You wouldn't want to know this:

At Caesar's victory celebrations in Rome, 2,000 war-captives, 400 lions, 200 horses, 20 elephants and many top gladiators fought and died – as entertainment.

No turning back now! We're going to rule Rome!

After he had conquered Gaul (France and Belgium) in 49 BC, Rome's Senate (governing council) ordered Caesar to return, alone. But Caesar disobeyed, and took his army with him. With their support, he was unstoppable!

Be prepared!
Always expect the very worst

Empire adventures

Whilst expanding his empire, Caesar claimed to fall in love with Egypt's Queen Cleopatra. Did he admire her beauty –or just want to win her kingdom?

Red = Roman Empire

BRITAIN

GERMANY

Black Sea

FRANCE

ITALY

GREECE

Rome

SPAIN

Mediterranean Sea

NORTH AFRICA

Wars in Gaul

No-one knows how many men died fighting Caesar's troops in Gaul, but Roman historians claimed that a million tribesmen were slaughtered and that a million were captured and sold as slaves.

Where are you taking us? Have we won something?

Who dares loses...

King Vercingetorix led the Gauls to rebel against Roman rule in 42 BC. But Caesar forced him to surrender, and he was taken to Rome, paraded through the streets, then executed – horribly.

'Veni, Vidi, Vici'?

(Latin: 'I came, I saw, I conquered!') Old stories say that those were Caesar's words when he invaded Britain in 55–54 BC. In fact, Caesar never said them – and he failed to conquer Britain. But these old stories tell us what people thought about his proud, confident character.

Retreat!

Samurai

Warrior monk Benkei hoped to make a magic sword from the tips of 1,000 others. So he prowled along Gojo Bridge, fighting any Samurai who dared to cross it. He killed 999 warriors, and took their weapons, but then the young soldier Yoshitsune defeated him. The two became comrades for the rest of their lives, fighting – and dying – together.

Vital Statistics ~ Benkei

Name:	Saitō Musashibō Benkei
Nickname:	Benkei
Born:	Japan
Lived:	1155 to 1189
Career:	Warrior monk
Fought:	Alongside famous Samurai (noble warrior) Yoshitsune

You wouldn't want to know this:

Benkei was said to be a 'demon child', with sharp, pointed teeth and long hair. He grew to be over 2 metres tall!

He's too quick! I can't catch him, even with my *naginata!**

Grr!

* killer blade fixed to a long pole.

Be prepared!
Always expect the very worst

Charge!

Wet, wet, wet

In 1184, enemies destroyed the only bridge over which Yoshitsune and Benkei could escape to safety after a battle. With amazing courage, they rode into the raging river – and survived to reach the other side.

I hope I don't lose my shoes...

What a way to go!

Shot full of enemy arrows while defending a castle, Benkei died on his feet, fighting bravely. Strangely, his body stayed standing for many hours afterwards. No-one dared approach it.

One more way to frighten the enemy! They'll think I'm a ghost!

Vital Statistics ~ Yoshitsune

Name: Minamoto no Yoshitsune
Nickname: Ushiwaka-maru (young ox)
Born: Japan
Lived: 1159 to 1189
Career: The most famous warrior of his age
Died: Killed himself to avoid the shame of defeat

You wouldn't want to know this:

After Yoshitsune died, his head was cut off, pickled in sake (Japanese rice wine) and sent to the leader of his enemies.

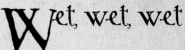

83

The Big Scream!

No 36

Attila the Hun

'The Terror of all Europe!' For fifteen frightful years, warlord Attila led Hun tribes to attack and destroy. The Huns swept away what peaceful citizens valued most – towns, churches, art, sports, music, farms, workshops, markets, family life and the chance to earn a living. But the Huns got what they came to find – land, loot and money.

Vital Statistics

Name: Attila (Father of his People)
Nickname: Scourge (Punishment) of God
Born: Hungary
Lived: AD 406 – 453
Career: Overlord of nomad tribes, known as 'Huns'
Fought: Europe, Central Asia
Died: In bed, on his wedding night, from a nosebleed.

You wouldn't want to know this:

At first, Attila shared power with his brother. But then he killed him, so that he could rule alone.

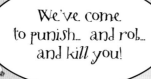

We've come to punish... and rob... and kill you!

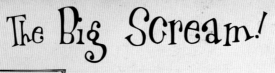

Be prepared!
Always expect the very worst

Destroyers!

In AD 435, Attila and his Huns attacked eastern Europe, spreading death and destruction. They wrecked 70 great cities, looting churches full of holy treasures and massacring priests, monks and nuns.

The Huns defeated Roman armies close to the Roman city of Constantinople (now Istanbul) in AD 443. The Romans paid Attila 2,000 kg of gold to go away, but he wanted more...

Fighting for food

From AD 451 to 452, Attila led his Huns westwards, towards Rome. His army destroyed all farm crops and livestock so that the Romans would starve. But when the Huns also ran short of food, Attila retreated, and died, unexpectedly, in bed.

You don't get to eat...

AD 451

Gaul

Western Roman Empire

AD 452

Rome

Gulp!

...and you don't get to live!

Napoleon

Genius or madman? No-one could be sure! From humble beginnings, Napoleon used ruthless warrior skills and supreme self-confidence to become Emperor of France. He won many famous victories, but he did not know when to stop fighting. His wars almost bankrupted France, and killed six million French and enemy soldiers.

Vital Statistics

Name: Napoleon Bonaparte
Nickname: 'Boney'
Born: Corsica (an island in the Mediterranean Sea)
Lived: 1769 to 1821
Career: Army commander; Emperor of France
Fought: To conquer all Europe – and beyond
Died: In prison, from illness or maybe accidental poisoning

You wouldn't want to know this:

Napoleon's enemies claimed that he ate naughty children!

One day glory, the next, disaster...

We're dying of cold and hunger! Curse you!

Be prepared!
Always expect the very worst

There is no such word as 'impossible'!

Breaking the rules

Napoleon became famous for his courage and daring. He won many battles using risky shortcuts and surprise manoeuvres. When invading Italy in 1796, he told his troops to 'move quickly and be ruthless about it'.

Napoleon's Empire

Between 1799 and 1814, Napoleon won control of Europe. But after he was defeated by Britain and its allies at the Battle of Waterloo (1815), French power collapsed quickly.

Look out! Enemy approaching!

The french advantage

Napoleon's troops were better organised and more highly trained than any previous French army. They also had more accurate cannon, and swift horse-drawn gun-carriages to rush them into battle. They even used hot-air balloons for spying.

No 38

Richard I and Saladin

Richard the Lionheart and Saladin – one Christian, one Muslim. These two warriors each believed that they were fighting for God. They led rival armies during the Third Crusade – a war between European and Middle Eastern powers for the holy city of Jerusalem. Richard and Saladin never met face to face, but they admired each other's courage and fighting skills.

Vital statistics

Name:	Yūsuf ibn Ayyūbi
Nickname:	Salah ad-Dīn / Saladin
Born:	Iraq
Lived:	1138 to 1193
Career:	Sultan (ruler)
Fought:	To capture Jerusalem. Succeeded in 1187.
Died:	Of fever, in Syria

You wouldn't want to know this:

Saladin was famously merciful. But he did kill top Christian knights, his most dangerous enemies.

A clever way to kill

In 1187, at the Battle of Hattin, Saladin set fire to the dry grass and bushes around a marching Crusader army, which dazed and confused them. The next day they were no match for Saladin's soldiers. Over 10,000 Crusaders were killed.

It is not the custom of kings to kill kings.

Be prepared!
Always expect the very worst

Cash for a Crusade

To pay for his army, Richard made the English pay heavy, unfair taxes, nicknamed the 'Saladin Tithe', and sold top government jobs to anyone who would pay. He even said, 'I will sell London if I can find a buyer.'

Ching!

Vital statistics

Name: Richard I/Richard Plantagenet
Nickname: The Lionheart
Born: England
Lived: 1157 to 1199
Career: King of England
Fought: To defeat Saladin in the Holy Land. Succeeded in 1191.
Died: Shot by a sniper at a French castle.

You wouldn't want to know this:

Richard ruled lands in France so ruthlessly that the people there rebelled against him.

Rough justice

Saladin was often merciful, but he could also be ruthless. In 1187, he captured Raynald of Châtillon – a very nasty character who attacked peaceful merchants, religious pilgrims and farmers. Although Raynald begged for his life, Saladin beheaded him.

After capturing the city of Acre in 1191, Richard had nearly 3,000 Muslim hostages killed – even though he had promised them safety. Why so ruthless? He couldn't take them into battle – and dared not risk leaving them behind.

I want to make the whole world tremble!

Alexander the Great

Small, stout, strong-willed, hot-tempered but utterly charming, Alexander's personality and ruthless ambition made him the greatest army commander. Who else could have persuaded troops to follow him 'to the ends of the earth'? He relied on cleverness and careful planning – not brute force – to win, and he never lost a battle!

Alexander was born with a twisted neck, so he was always gazing upwards.

A god among men – that's me!

Vital Statistics

Name: Alexander III
Nickname: The Great
Born: Macedonia
Lived: 356 to 323 BC
Career: King of Macedonia; army commander
Fought: To conquer the world
Died: In Babylon (Iraq), perhaps poisoned

You wouldn't want to know this:

In a fury, Alexander set fire to the magnificent capital city of the mighty Persian empire (now Iran and the nearby lands). It was completely destroyed.

After conquering Egypt in 332 BC, Alexander visited the temple of Amun, the Sun-God. There, an oracle declared him the 'son of the god', 'master of the universe' and also Pharaoh of Egypt.

Be prepared!
Always expect the very worst

Aged just 13, Alexander tamed a mighty warhorse, Bucephalus. He saw that the horse was frightened by its own shadow, and gently turned it to face the sun.

To the ends of the earth

Map labels: SOGDIANA, Caspian Sea, MACEDONIA, Black Sea, Gordion, BACTRIA, GREECE, MESOPOTAMIA, Babylon, PERSIA, INDIA, Tyre, SYRIA, Persepolis, Alexandria, BABYLONIA, Persian Gulf, Indian Ocean, EGYPT, Red Sea

Knotty problem

When Alexander visited Gordion in 333 BC, he saw an ancient knot that no-one could untie – and sliced straight through it! A prophecy said that the first man to free the knot would become king of Asia.

Chop

After conquering Greece, the Balkans and Egypt, Alexander's army headed east, into unknown, hostile territory. He overpowered the splendid Persian Empire, together with many smaller kingdoms, until his troops reached India.

final frontier

Alexander was not all-powerful. When he reached the River Hyphasis in India, the water was deep and fast-flowing, and Indian armies with fierce war-elephants waited on the other side. His men turned back, refusing to go further.

Glark!

What's that?! A monster?!

Hrrrrrmmmmphh!

Genghis Khan

While he lived, and for centuries after, Genghis Khan was probably the most feared man on Earth. He was certainly its most ruthless destroyer – over 40 million men, women and children were killed by his armies. But Genghis was also the first to unite and organise the Mongol tribes of Central Asia, and he led them to conquer the largest empire the world had ever seen.

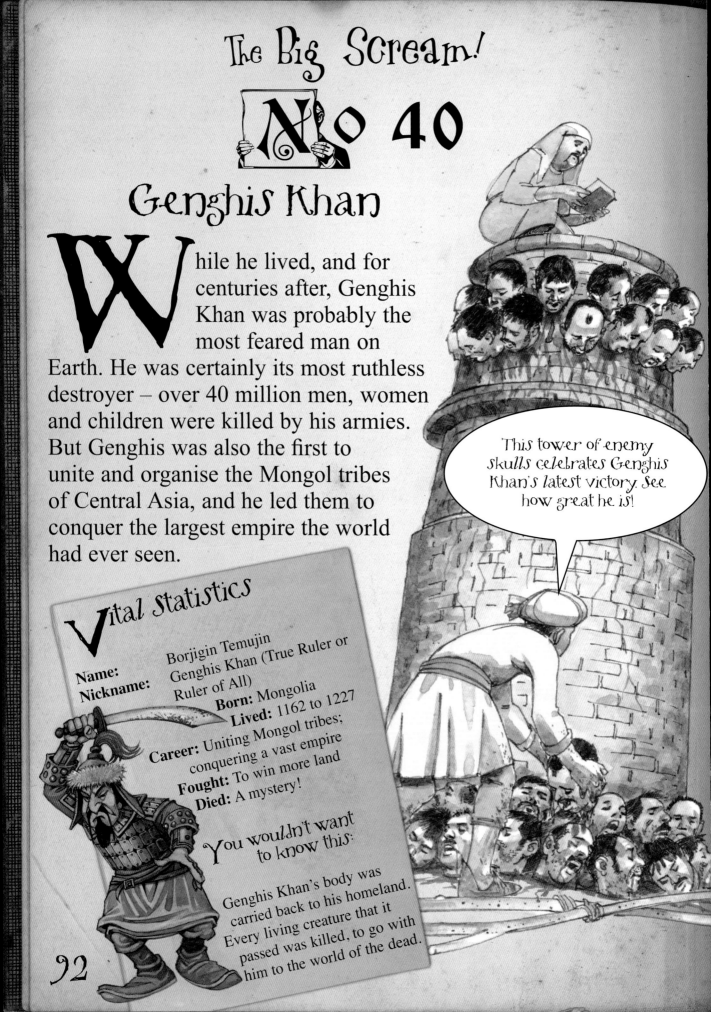

This tower of enemy skulls celebrates Genghis Khan's latest victory. See how great he is!

Vital Statistics

Name: Borjigin Temujin
Nickname: Genghis Khan (True Ruler or Ruler of All)
Born: Mongolia
Lived: 1162 to 1227
Career: Uniting Mongol tribes; conquering a vast empire
Fought: To win more land
Died: A mystery!

You wouldn't want to know this:

Genghis Khan's body was carried back to his homeland. Every living creature that it passed was killed, to go with him to the world of the dead.

Be prepared!
Always expect the very worst

> If anyone can, Genghis Khan!

Hit and run

Mongol warriors fought on horseback, galloping up to enemies and firing arrows. They besieged cities with giant catapults and battering rams. If the citizens surrendered and paid a ransom, they were usually allowed to live – in fear of the next Mongol attack!

Serves them right?!

Anyone who dared oppose Genghis Khan was cruelly punished. He murdered one enemy leader by pouring molten metal into his eyes and ears. Others were crushed to death.

> So that's what heavy metal sounds like!

Timur

Genghis Khan had many wives and children, and we can still trace his descendants today. One was Timur Lenk (lived 1336 to 1405), an ambitious ruler of Central Asia who was chosen to lead after winning a hat-throwing game that tested his aiming skills. He died trying to conquer China.

fwoosh!

Genghis Khan's Empire

Awesome empire

In just 21 years, from 1206 to 1227, Genghis Khan took control of lands stretching from the Pacific Ocean to the Caspian Sea. His conquests created new laws, nations, ways of writing, the first banknotes and, through terror of Mongol punishments, long-lasting peace.

Nº 41

Captain Kidd

British privateer William Kidd was licensed to attack the French, and pirates. In 1698, he captured the magnificent *Quedah Merchant*. It flew a French flag, but came from India. Furious Indian princes accused Kidd of piracy, and the English agreed. Kidd's crew deserted him; he sailed away to hide.

Vital Statistics

Name:	William Kidd
Nickname:	'Captain Kidd'
Lived:	1645 to 1701
Born:	Scotland
Career:	Privateer, pirate
Sailed:	Caribbean, Indian Ocean
Died:	Hanged

You wouldn't want to know this:

Kidd was hanged twice! The first time, the hangman's rope broke, and he survived. So they hanged him again!

Not guilty?

In 1699, Kidd was captured in Boston (now in the USA) and shipped to London, where he was sentenced to death for piracy. But was he really guilty?

Betrayed!

Wealthy politicians from England and Ireland had secretly financed Kidd's privateering voyage. In return, they expected a generous share of his booty. But when the English government put Kidd on trial, these backers disowned him, to protect their own political careers. If they had spoken up for Kidd, he might have been pardoned and set free.

Buried treasure

After Kidd died, people wondered where he had buried his loot from the *Quedah Merchant*. Rumours said that it was hidden on Long Island, now part of New York. But treasure-hunters have never found it!

Warning

Kidd's body was coated in pitch (sticky, waterproof tar), put in an iron cage, and hung by the docks at Tilbury, near London. It gave a grisly greeting to sailors and pirates.

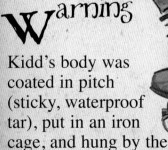

№ 42

Sweyn Asliefsson

Good friends, a fertile farm, a big house and a fine family – Sweyn Asleifsson had everything! How did he get it? Mostly by fighting, looting and killing! Sweyn was a typical Viking pirate. He fought to win fame and glory, to protect his family from bloody feuds, to win riches – and, according to Viking poets – because he enjoyed it.

Vital Statistics

Name: Sweyn Asleifsson
Lived: c. 1120 to 1160
Born: Orkney Islands (between Scotland and Norway)
Career: Pirate and raider
Sailed: Scotland, Ireland, Wales
Died: Of natural causes, at home

You wouldn't want to know this:

Sweyn and Rosta were bitter Viking enemies. In 1139, Sweyn burned down Rosta's house, even though he knew that Rosta's family was trapped inside.

Raiders from the sea!

Yaarrgh!

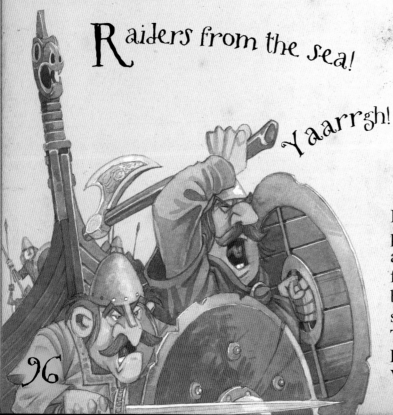

In fine weather, Viking pirates raided peaceful coastal villages, monasteries and markets. They sailed their fast, sleek dragon-ships up onto a beach, then leaped out, brandishing sharp swords and brutal battle-axes. Terrified villagers hid, or ran away. Raids were a bloody business; the Vikings showed no mercy!

Be prepared!
Always expect the very worst

Loot!

Viking pirates grabbed anything they could sell: gold and silver from churches, furs and amber from traders – and young men and women, to be used as slaves.

What the sagas say ...

According to a poem called the 'Orkneyinga Saga', written in Iceland around AD 1200, Sweyn spent his year this way:

- Winter: at home with his warriors

- Early spring: planting crops on his farm

- Late spring: raiding Ireland and the Scottish Islands

- Summer: on his farm, harvesting crops

- Autumn: sailing on more pirate raids

Bloody love

In 1140, Sweyn sailed south, chasing pirates from Wales. Landing on the Isle of Man, he met a beautiful, sorrowful woman – Welsh pirates had just killed her husband. She agreed to marry Sweyn, but only after he had caught and killed all her husband's murderers.

Sweyn boasted that he could entertain 80 warriors for a whole winter. They passed the dark Orkney days and nights in his great hall, eating, drinking and telling stories of their adventures.

97

Anne Bonny and Mary Read

Women are trouble! That's what pirate captains said, and most sailors agreed with them. They complained that females brought bad luck, or made crewmen jealous and quarrelsome. Everyone knew that women could not fight or sail a ship – and everyone was amazed when two particularly cruel, clever pirates turned out to be women! Their names were Anne Bonny and Mary Read.

Vital Statistics

Name:	Anne Bonny
Born:	County Cork, Ireland
Career:	Pirate
Lived:	1697 (some say 1682) to 1721
Sailed:	Caribbean
Died:	Unknown
Name:	Mary Read
Born:	Plymouth, England
Career:	Pirate
Lived:	c. 1690 to 1721
Sailed:	Caribbean
Died:	Of fever, in gaol

Sharing tasks with sailors

It's not all plunder and treasure, you know.

To stay safe on board ship, Anne and Mary hid the fact that they were women from all the other sailors. Bloodthirsty, brave and extremely tough, they worked as hard as all the men, and were famed for their most 'unladylike' fierceness, swearing and bad temper.

Be prepared!
Always expect the very worst

Runaway lovers

Anne Cormac emigrated from Ireland to America. There, she married James Bonny, a failed pirate (and a spy), but was unhappy. She fell in love with another pirate, 'Calico Jack' Rackham, and ran away with him. Together, they cruised the Caribbean, plundering ships and taking prisoners – including Mary Read – to sell as slaves.

Always in disguise

Young Mary Read worked as a page and a ship's cabin boy, to earn money for her mother. Still dressed in male clothes, she joined the English army, married a soldier, and helped him run an inn. After he died, Mary went back to sea, was captured by Calico Jack, and became a pirate.

Calico Jack

Nicknamed 'Calico Jack' for the fine cotton shirts he wore, Rackham was much less brave than Read or Bonny. He refused to fight when the British navy attacked his ship, was arrested, and found guilty. Bonny was scornful:

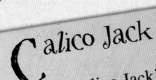

If you had fought like a man you needn't have hang'd like a dog.

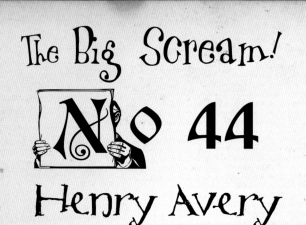

№44

Henry Avery

A lifelong sailor, Henry Avery went to sea as a boy on English navy ships. Seeking quick riches, he became a slave-trader in West Africa, enslaving the merchants who sold slaves to him. Popular, and a born leader, he became a pirate after leading a mutiny against an English captain. Then he headed far east, and struck amazingly lucky! He captured the Mughal emperor's ship, *Ganj-i-Sawai*, laden with fabulous treasures.

Vital Statistics

Name: Henry Avery (or Every)
Nickname: 'Long Ben'
Lived: *c.* 1653 to *c.* 1699
Born: Devon, England
Career: Pirate
Sailed: Indian Ocean
Died: Fate unknown

You wouldn't want to know this:

There were hundreds of women on board the Mughal treasure ship. Many killed themselves, rather than be attacked by Avery's pirates.

Whack!

Be prepared!
Always expect the very worst

Deadly pirate weapons

Cutlass – *a sharp, broad-bladed, butcher's knife. First used by buccaneers.*

Bombs – *pots or bottles filled with a mixture of smoky explosives and killer lead shot.*

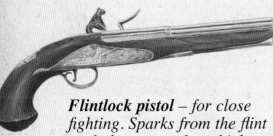

Flintlock pistol – *for close fighting. Sparks from the flint explode gunpowder which shoots heavy lead balls.*

Chain-shot – *empty cannonball cases, joined by a chain, will soon cut through enemy ships' rigging.*

Death flag

Henry Avery may have been the first to fly the 'Skull and Crossbones' flag. Sometimes called the 'Jolly Roger', this was a sign that pirates would show no mercy. So was a plain red '*Jolie Rouge*' (pretty red) flag.

Each pirate captain had his own version of the Jolly Roger:

Christopher Moody   *Blackbeard*   *Jack Rackham*

Edward Low   *Bartholomew Roberts*   *Thomas Tew*

The greatest prize ever

The *Ganj-i-Sawai* was the richest prize ever captured by a pirate. A huge dhow (cargo ship), with valuable guns, she carried priceless pearls, precious stones, and half a million coins of solid gold and silver, as well as other treasures – including a saddle encrusted with real rubies!

Sir Henry Morgan

The Spanish Main was a very dangerous place. But young Henry Morgan went there, keen to win fame and fortune by fighting against Spain. He was sent on secret missions by the English to attack Spanish settlements, leading shiploads of savage buccaneers.

In 1671, he destroyed Panama, a peaceful Spanish city, and was sent home in disgrace. But England needed his skills and knowledge, so he was pardoned and ended his career as Governor of Jamaica.

Vital Statistics

Name:	Sir Henry Morgan
Nickname:	'Captain Blood'
Lived:	c. 1635 to 1688
Born:	Wales
Career:	Buccaneer leader
Sailed:	Caribbean
Died:	Peacefully, from illness

You wouldn't want to know this:

When attacking Spanish settlements, Morgan used priests, nuns and even children as 'human shields' and hostages.

What are you looking at?

Buccaneers were runaway slaves, starving settlers, criminals, pirates and outlaws. They lived rough on Hispaniola (now Haiti) and dressed in home-made, smelly, blood-stained animal hides.

Be prepared!
Always expect the very worst

Pirate punishments

- **Bilboes** – These iron hoops, fastened round your ankles, will trap you on deck.

- **Cat-o'-nine-tails** – This whip has nine strands ('tails') studded with knots or fish hooks. It can kill.

- **Ducking** – You'll be tied to a rope and dipped into the sea. You might drown!

- **Keel-hauling** – You'll be thrown overboard and dragged under the keel. It's covered with barnacles; they'll skin you alive – and you'll die!

One punishment you'll avoid is 'walking the plank' – being forced along a strip of wood and into the sea. This way of killing was probably dreamed up by later writers; real pirates didn't do it.

Cat-o'-nine-tails

How buccaneers got their name

When not at sea, the wild bunch on Hispaniola hunted pigs and cattle and sold meat, fat and hides to passing ships. Local Arawak people taught them how to preserve the meat in a *boucan* – the French word for 'smokehouse' (settlers came from many parts of Europe). Soon, the hunters had a nickname: *boucaniers* (smokers). In English, this became 'buccaneers'.

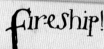

Fireship!

In 1669, Morgan's buccaneers made a daring attack at Maracaibo, Venezuela. They filled hollow logs with gunpowder, loaded them on an empty ship, sailed it close to the Spanish fleet – then lit the fuses!

№ 46

Sir Francis Drake

Master mariner, royal favourite and world explorer, Drake rose from humble origins to become England's national hero. Raised on a houseboat, he learned seafaring skills from his uncle, a ruthless slave-trader. Proud nobles despised Drake, but his courage helped defeat the Spanish Armada in 1588. And his privateering exploits won fabulous riches.

Vital Statistics

Name: Francis Drake
Nickname: El Draque (the Dragon)
Born: Devon, England
Lived: *c.* 1540 to 1596
Career: Explorer, slave-trader, privateer
Sailed: Spanish Main; Pacific Ocean; round the world
Died: Of dysentery, in the Caribbean

You wouldn't want to know this:

On his round-the-world voyage, Drake quarrelled with his second-in-command, and had him hanged. But the night before, Drake entertained him to dinner in a most friendly fashion – and that was after passing sentence!

Spanish gold

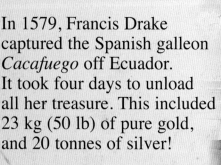

Golden ornaments from South America

Every year, Spanish galleons laden with gold and silver mined in South America sailed from Panama back home to Spain.

In 1579, Francis Drake captured the Spanish galleon *Cacafuego* off Ecuador. It took four days to unload all her treasure. This included 23 kg (50 lb) of pure gold, and 20 tonnes of silver!

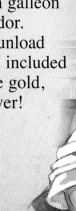

Be prepared!
Always expect the very worst
Take care in the 'Spanish Main'

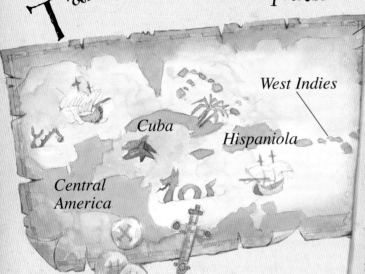

Map of the Spanish Main

West Indies

Cuba

Hispaniola

Central America

The seas around Spanish settlements in South America were known as the 'Spanish Main'. Pirates and privateers from many European countries prowled the seas there, eager to attack Spanish treasure-ships.

Queen Elizabeth I of England took a secret interest in Drake's privateering adventures. Around 1570, she gave him 'letters of marque' – written permission – to attack treasure ships from Spain.

When Drake returned to England in 1581, after his historic voyage round the world, he brought enough pirate treasure with him to repay all the English government's debts – and buy himself a splendid mansion. As a reward, Queen Elizabeth I made him a knight.

Navigation

Like all pirate captains, it was Drake's task to navigate his ship through unknown waters. To find its position out of sight of land, Drake measured time passing, the ship's speed, its compass bearing, and the height of the sun. He then plotted (recorded) this information in logbooks and on traverse boards.

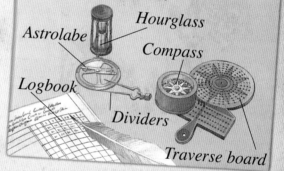

Hourglass

Astrolabe

Compass

Logbook

Dividers

Traverse board

Arise, Sir Francis!

№ 47

The Barbarossa Brothers

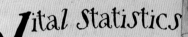

T he Barbary Coast of North Africa was home to a rich, elegant Muslim civilisation. But most Europeans did not know or care. They simply feared Barbary pirates! The most famous and successful, Horuk and Heyreddin Barbarossa, won wars against Christian Spain, conquered kingdoms for Turkey, and helped thousands of Muslim refugees escape to safety. Heyreddin also commanded the Turkish Navy.

Vital Statistics

Name:	Horuk
Nickname:	'Barbarossa' (Red Beard)
Lived:	1473 to 1518
Born:	Greece
Career:	Pirate
Sailed:	Mediterranean Sea
Died:	Executed by the Spanish
Name:	Heyreddin
Nickname:	'Barbarossa' (Red Beard – he dyed it to copy his brother)
Lived:	1475 to 1546
Born:	Greece
Career:	Pirate, Ottoman (Turkish) admiral
Sailed:	Mediterranean Sea
Died:	Of old age

You wouldn't want to know this:

In just one year, 1544, Heyreddin Barbarossa captured 9,000 Christians and sold them as slaves.

Barbary pirates sailed in galleys – warships rowed by slaves. Galley-slaves were convicted criminals, or pirates' captives. Their lives were terrible. Chained to their seats, they were whipped to make them row faster.

The fight against Barbary Pirates was led by corsairs (privateers) from Malta. Commanded by Christian knights, they fought against Islam, but were also keen to capture Muslim ships' valuable cargoes.

Be prepared!
Always expect the very worst

How to avoid Barbary pirates

• If you're travelling to the holy city of Jerusalem, go overland if possible. It takes longer than by sea, but it's safer.

• If you have heavy cargoes to transport, and must cross the Mediterranean Sea, make sure that your vessel is protected by soldiers and warships.

• Steer north if you can. The Barbary pirates live on the southern shores of the Mediterranean. It's easier for them to raid close at home.

Fighting at sea

Soldier of fortune

Sir Francis Verney (lived 1584 to 1615) was an English gentleman who became a Muslim and lived in Algiers, North Africa. For six years, he grew rich as a Barbary pirate. But he was captured by Christians, sold as a slave, and died soon after.

Human muscle-power plus special triangular sails made galleys fast and easy to steer: ideal for attacks on slower cargo ships.

Barbary pirate ships carried troops of janissaries (trained soldiers), ready to leap onto enemy ships and overpower the crew.

In battle, galleys rowed quickly towards sailing ships, smashing holes in their hulls and sinking them. Crews were forced to surrender – or leap overboard and drown.

No 48

Zheng Yi Sao

Young and beautiful, Shi Xianggu wed pirate captain Zheng Yi. He commanded the largest Chinese fleet of his time. With 800 junks, 1,000 smaller ships and 75,000 sailors, it may have been the greatest pirate fleet ever.

When Zheng Yi died in a tropical storm, Shi took over his pirate empire – and his name. Everyone called her 'Zheng Yi Sao' (Zheng Yi's Widow). Her ships raided across the South China Seas, robbing, destroying and demanding taxes. In 1810, the Chinese government pardoned Zheng Yi Sao for her crimes. She married her dead husband's adopted son and gave up piracy, for ever.

Vital Statistics

Name: Shi Xianggu
Nickname: 'Zheng Yi Sao' (Zheng Yi's Widow)
Born: South China
Lived: 1775 or 1785 to 1844
Career: Pirate
Sailed: China Seas
Died: At home, of old age

You wouldn't want to know this:

If one of Zheng Yi Sao's crew left her ship without permission, his ear was cut off as punishment.

Keeping control

Get to work, NOW!

As a woman pirate, Zheng Yi Sao had to be tougher than any man. She was famous for harsh punishments handed out to pirates who disobeyed her.

Be prepared!
Always expect the very worst

For fighting on board enemy ships, Chinese pirates chose long, heavy swords. They were so sharp that they could slice through metal.

Chinese pirates sailed in converted junks (cargo vessels). Fast, seaworthy, armed with cannons, and with big holds to store gunpowder, junks were ideal for fighting.

Chinese junk

Gunboat power

To protect its profitable opium trade, the British government sent Royal Navy gunboats to attack Chinese pirates. In 1849, soon after Zheng Yi Sao died, they destroyed Chinese pirates' power for ever, by blowing up their ships at the mouth of the Haiphong River (now in Vietnam).

Doubly successful

After Zheng Yi Sao retired from pirate raiding, she began a second money-making career. She ran a gambling house in Guangzhou, and died a very rich woman!

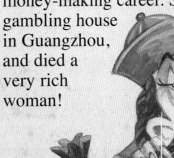

Bartholomew Roberts

Famous for wanting 'a short life and a merry one', Roberts was one of the most successful pirates ever. In just two years, he captured 400 ships, winning 'pleasure, liberty and power'. In spite of his brilliant – and cruel – career, Roberts did not plan to be a pirate. Originally third mate on a slave-trading ship, he was chosen as captain when its crew mutinied. Today he is remembered for the remarkable rules he created for pirates to follow.

Vital Statistics

Name:	John (later Bartholomew) Roberts
Nickname:	'Black Bart'
Born:	Wales
Lived:	1682 to 1722
Career:	Pirate, slave trader
Sailed:	Brazil, Newfoundland (Canada), Caribbean, West Africa
Died:	In battle

You wouldn't want to know this:

Roberts caused such fear that for a year (1720–1721) few ships dared sail in Caribbean waters.

Looking this good is hard work.

Dressed to kill

Roberts always put on his best clothes before battle: a velvet suit and a shirt trimmed with lace. Proud of his captain's rank, he wanted to encourage his men – and face death looking good.

Captain Roberts' rules

1. Fair shares of food and drink for all – and an equal vote on important decisions.

2. Equal shares of plunder for all crew.

3. Cheats to be marooned; onboard robbers to have noses and ears slit.

4. No gambling, dice or cards.

5. Early to bed – no candles below decks.

6. No wives or girlfriends on voyages.

7. People caught deserting ship to be punished by death or marooning.

8. No fights or duels among crewmen at sea.

9. Wounded pirates to get a pension.

10. Ship musicians to have rest on Sundays.

How to fire a cannon

1. Ram gunpowder into the barrel.

2. Add wad (a woollen pad) to keep gunpowder in position.

3. Add cannonball.

4. Secure cannonball with wad.

5. Set the gunpowder alight (by a match). It will explode and hurl the cannonball towards your enemies!

Barrel

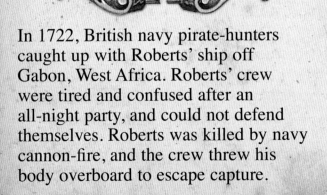

In 1722, British navy pirate-hunters caught up with Roberts' ship off Gabon, West Africa. Roberts' crew were tired and confused after an all-night party, and could not defend themselves. Roberts was killed by navy cannon-fire, and the crew threw his body overboard to escape capture.

No 50

Blackbeard

Most pirates were murderers. But Blackbeard chose a different way to win treasure, behaving like a 'fury from hell' to terrify sailors. This, plus the 40 cannons on his ship, forced victims to surrender. Blackbeard captured a rival pirate fleet, took control of Charleston port (now in South Carolina, USA), then began fresh adventures. British Navy ships cornered him. He endured 5 gunshot wounds and 20 sword-cuts before collapsing.

Vital Statistics

Name: Edward Teach
Nickname: 'Blackbeard'
Born: Bristol, England
Lived: c. 1680 to 1718
Career: Pirate
Sailed: Caribbean
How he died: In battle

You wouldn't want to know this:

Blackbeard's headless body is said to have swum seven times round his ship. Then it disappeared!

Before battle, Blackbeard fixed lighted gun-fuses under his hat. They surrounded him with devilish smoke. He also carried six pistols, all loaded.

Be prepared!
Always expect the very worst

Legendary lover?

Daddy!

Did Blackbeard's striking looks and international fame make him attractive to women? Rumours said he had at least 14 wives. But perhaps he invented these stories himself, to increase his reputation!

Gruesome guard

Blackbeard hid his treasure somewhere near Charleston – perhaps on a deserted island. Frightened sailors reported that he buried a murdered pirate on top of each treasure-chest, to scare robbers away.

Marooned!

To keep his treasure to himself, Blackbeard marooned his pirate crew on a lonely island. He left them with a day's supply of water, some brandy (as medicine), and a gun – to shoot themselves if they felt desperate! Unless marooned men found food and fresh water, they were doomed to die. Marooning was a popular way for pirate captains to punish mutineers or dispose of unwanted captives.

Marooned... I'm doomed!

Down to hell

Blackbeard tested new recruits to his crew by shutting them up in 'hell' – his ship's hold, full of smoke and fumes.

The Big Scream!

№ 51

Al Capone

Nicknamed 'Scarface' after getting slashed during a fight, Al Capone was the most feared gangster in America during the 1920s and 30s. His gang, the 'Capones', made their money from smuggling alcohol, which was illegal during the Prohibition years. They often battled other mobs in Chicago. Capone ordered the murder of many rivals and even killed some of them with his own hands.

Vital Statistics

Name:	Alphonse 'Al' Gabriel Capone
Alias:	'Scarface'
Lived:	1899 to 1947
Crimes:	Murder, smuggling, tax evasion.
Victims:	Dozens of rival gangsters.

You wouldn't want to know this:

One of Capone's victims took three hours to die. When asked who shot him, he replied, 'Nobody', despite having 14 bullet wounds!

When Capone found out members of his own gang were out to get him, he bashed them with a baseball bat, then had them shot.

Are you looking at me, wise guy?

Be prepared!
Always expect the very worst

St Valentine's Day massacre

In 1929, Capone hoped to ambush a rival gangster, Bugs Moran. On February 14, St Valentine's Day, five members of Moran's North Side gang and two other men turned up at a garage expecting to buy illegal drink. Dressed as police officers, Capone's mobsters lined them up against the wall – and gunned them down in a hail of bullets.

In the slammer

In 1929, FBI agent Eliot Ness began to investigate Capone. Two years later, Capone was finally sentenced to 11 years in prison – for not paying his taxes!

Nicknames

Can you guess how these gangsters got their nicknames?: Jimmy the Gent, Terry 'Machine Gun' Druggan, Vincent 'Mad Dog' Coll and Donald Angelini, 'The Wizard of Odds'. Tough guy 'Lucky' Luciano got his nickname after getting his throat cut, being left for dead in a ditch and somehow surviving!

Capone spent much of his time behind bars in the notorious Alcatraz prison in San Francisco Bay.

Making a swim for it?

Secret weapons

There's a popular myth that gangsters carried their machine guns in violin cases. It's probably untrue, but they did hide them: Capone kept a shotgun in a golf bag, while other mobsters hid them under folded newspapers.

POSSE BENT ON LYNCHING
SEARCHES WOODS FOR PREY

Chicago Defender

10¢

No 52

Dick Turpin

If you believe the legends, 'Dauntless' Dick Turpin was a handsome hero. Riding his noble steed Black Bess, he dashed along highways, robbing the rich and winning the hearts of ladies. The real Richard Turpin was a regular thief who tortured his female victims until they handed over their money and jewellery.

Contrary to legend, Dick Turpin's famous ride, from London to York in less than 24 hours, was actually made by 17th-century highwayman John 'Swift Nick' Nevison.

Vital Statistics

Name: Richard Turpin
Alias: 'Gentleman Highwayman'
Lived: c.1705 to 1739
Crimes: Highway robbery, burgling, stealing horses and sheep
Victims: He tortured many.

You wouldn't want to know this:

When a wealthy widow refused to tell Turpin where her money was hidden, he hoisted her over an open fire until she gave up her treasure.

Catch me if you can!

Gallop!

Be prepared!
Always expect the very worst

Stand and deliver!

The sheep stealer

Young Turpin started out stealing sheep and cattle to sell in his butcher's shop. After he was found out, he fled into the countryside where he formed the 'Essex Gang'. The gang attacked farmhouses and robbed the inhabitants. Later, Turpin began working with 'Captain' Tom King, a famous highwayman. From a hidden cave in Epping Forest, they robbed passers-by.

A graceful exit

One night lawmen tracked Turpin and King to a London pub. In the fight, Turpin accidentally shot his partner! Turpin headed north to York, where he was eventually arrested for stealing horses. Only on his way to the gallows did Turpin act like a hero, bowing to the crowds and chatting to his executioner.

Click!

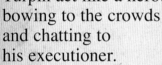

The flintlock was the first gun that fired almost instantly. Armed with this weapon, a lone highwayman could hold up a stagecoach.

The wicked lady

Highwaymen were mounted robbers who held up stagecoaches. Some did have a romantic streak: Frenchman Claude Duval danced with a lady during a hold-up near London in 1668. Lady Catherine Ferrers, known as the 'Wicked Lady', robbed coaches just for fun. After many daring hold-ups, she was finally shot by one of her victims in 1660.

Your money or your life!

117

Nº 53

Billy the Kid

Henry McCarty, or 'Billy the Kid', was a brutal Wild West outlaw who killed several men while still a teenager. Soon he was one of the most wanted men in the West. After his capture at Stinking Springs in 1880, he told a reporter: 'People thought me bad before, but if I ever get free, I'll let them know what bad means.' He became a legend after his captor, Sheriff Pat Garrett, wrote a best-selling book about him.

Vital Statistics

Name:
Alias: Henry McCarty
William Bonney or 'Billy the Kid'
Lived: 1859 to 1881
Crimes: Cattle rustling, murder, gambling
Victims: Murdered 4–9 people.

You wouldn't want to know this:

While escaping from prison, Billy grabbed a shotgun, then lay in wait for his captors. When deputy Robert Ollinger came running past, Billy shouted 'Hello Bob!' then blasted him with the shotgun. Billy then rode out of town, reportedly singing.

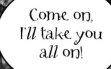

Come on, I'll take you all on!

Be prepared!
Always expect the very worst
Dead or alive

In the wide open spaces of the Wild West, it wasn't always easy to capture villains. So criminals were made into 'outlaws'. This meant anyone could bring them in: 'Dead or Alive'. Most were just robbers or murderers but some, such as Butch Cassidy, were turned into heroes in books and films.

WANTED

DEAD OR ALIVE

$1,000

In cold blood

It's said that Billy carried out his first murder at just 12, stabbing a man in a saloon fight. Later, when his ranch boss was killed in a gang feud, Billy set out on a bloody trail of murder and cattle-rustling.

Eventually Billy was hunted down by Sheriff Pat Garrett to a house in New Mexico. Garrett ambushed Billy and shot him dead. Billy was just 21.

Woah!

Bang!

Son of a gun!

Many Wild West outlaws had nicknames, like 'Big Nose' George Parrot or Thomas 'Black Jack' Ketchum, while Harvey Logan was called 'Kid Curry'. Gangs had names as well. Billy the Kid was one of the 'Regulators'. Butch Cassidy and the Sundance Kid (real names Harry Longbaugh and Robert Leroy Parker) were members of the 'Wild Bunch'.

It was a race to draw our guns – and I got there first!

I can sniff danger a mile off!

No 54

Ned Kelly

Ned Kelly is Australia's most famous bandit. But though he was a bank robber who shot several policemen, some say he was only defending himself. The Kelly gang famously built suits of bulletproof armour. When the police first saw it, one of them cried out 'Look out, boys, it's the bunyip!' (a mythical lake monster). But Kelly's armour did not save him from the hangman. His last words were: 'Such is life!'

Vital Statistics

Name: Edward Kelly
Alias: 'Ned'
Lived: 1855 to 1880
Crimes: Cattle rustling, murder, robbery
Victims: He shot three dead.

You wouldn't want to know this:

The Kelly gang often took hostages who were only set free if their demands were met. In the final shoot-out, several hostages were shot, and three died, including 13-year-old Jack Jones. But on another occasion, the outlaws entertained their prisoners with a display of horse riding and tricks.

Give it your best shot. I'm bulletproof!

Be prepared!
Always expect the very worst

Bushrangers

Australia's most feared bandits were the bushrangers. Most were convicts or outlaws who had escaped into the bush, Australia's wilderness. They robbed farmers and travellers with the cry 'Bail up!' This meant 'halt', as cows were held still by putting 'bails' (frames) around their neck.

Bail up!

Robin Hoods?

Nineteenth-century songs called 'ballads' made the bushrangers into brave heroes. Ned Kelly and Frederick Ward, alias 'Captain Thunderbolt', were seen as Robin Hoods, robbing from the rich to help the poor. 'Captain Thunderbolt', famous for his fast horse, preferred to escape from trouble rather than get into a shootout.

Zoom!

On the run

As a young man, Ned Kelly often got into trouble with the police. Accused of wounding a police officer, Ned, his brother and two friends fled into the bush. When the police tracked him down, Ned shot three of them dead. His gang were now outlaws. He led them in two bank raids, sharing the money with his family and neighbours.

When the police finally caught up with the Kelly gang on 28 June 1880, they fired 15,000 bullets into the inn where the gang were hiding. The bullets bounced off Kelly's armour, until he was shot in the legs. He was arrested and hanged for murder soon afterwards.

Sorry, it's for the mammy!

121

N₀ 55

Jesse James

One of the most notorious outlaws of the Wild West was Jesse James. In 1867 he robbed his first bank, and six years later his gang held up their first train. He once held up two stagecoaches in one day. Many poor farmers hated the banks and railroads he stole from, so Jesse James became a legend. But was he really such a hero?

Vital Statistics

Name: Jesse Woodson James
Alias: 'Dingus'
Lived: 1847 to 1882
Crimes: Horse stealing, train and bank robbery, murder
Victims: 14 dead

You wouldn't want to know this:

A five-year-old girl was once trampled to death while Jesse James was robbing a ticket booth at the Missouri State Fair.

Tickets, please!

Be prepared!
Always expect the very worst

Blown sky-high!

Train robbers often picked a quiet spot where the train slowed down. Riding up on horses, one of them jumped onto the moving train then unhitched the rail cars with the loot in them. Once, the Wild Bunch used too much dynamite to crack the safe. They blew up the whole car, sending $30,000 of cash into the air!

Room for two

Jesse James first became famous in 1869 after he robbed a bank in Gallatin, Missouri and killed the cashier. Now outlaws, Jesse and his brother Frank made a daring escape by riding off on the same horse.

A bungled job

During a raid on Northfield, Minnesota in 1876, the cashiers refused to hand over the money. Outside, five of the James gang were shot in a gun battle with the locals. But James soon formed a new gang. In 1881 he robbed four more trains.

Soon Jesse's new gang fell out and the only people he trusted were two brothers, Charley and Robert Ford. Bad move. Bob shot Jesse in the head while he was hanging a picture, then claimed the reward!

Sorry, Jesse.

Click!

123

No 56

Sawney Bean

Sawney Bean was a Scottish bandit said to live with his large family in a cave by the sea. For 25 years, their supplies came from robbing passing travellers at night – and their food came from eating them! The Beans were sneaky. They never attacked more than two travellers at a time, then they mobbed their victims so there was no escape.

Vital Statistics

Name: Alexander 'Sawney' Bean
Alias: 'The Cannibal Bandit'
Lived: 16th century
Crimes: Robbery, murder
Victims: Pot loads

You wouldn't want to know this:

Legend says that Sawney Bean was the head of a 'cursed tribe' of killers, including his wife, eight sons, six daughters, 18 grandsons and 14 grand-daughters!

Something I ate disagreed with me!

Yes, your last victim!

The Donner Party

There have been several cases of people eating each other when supplies ran low. In the winter of 1846–1847, a group of American pioneers known as the Donner (not dinner!) Party munched each other after getting caught in the snow in the Sierra Nevada mountains of California.

Gosh! Something's afoot!

After murdering their victims, the Beans brought the bodies back to the cave and cut them up. Leftover parts were sometimes thrown into the sea. When the tide washed up arms and legs, people wondered who had carried out this terrible crime.

I hope you smell 'em before I do!

Sniff

When the tide was in, the water flowed deep into the Beans' cave, so no-one knew anyone lived there.

Napkin, anyone?

Caught red-handed!

One night, a group of fairgoers caught the Beans in the middle of an ambush. King James VI of Scotland is said to have sent out 400 men and several bloodhounds, who found the Beans' cave littered with human remains. The whole family was taken away and executed!

No 59

The Blood Countess

One of the cruellest women that ever lived, the Hungarian Countess Elizabeth Báthory is said to have killed dozens, if not hundreds, of young women. Rumours spread that Báthory was a vampire who drank her victims' blood as well as bathing in it. Both stories are probably untrue. She was just a vicious villain who was rich and powerful enough to get away with murder.

Vital Statistics

Name: Countess Elizabeth Báthory de Ecsed
Alias: The 'Blood Countess'
Lived: 1560 to 1614
Crimes: Murder, torture
Victims: Between 80 and 650. No-one knows for sure!

You wouldn't want to know this:

In one version of the story, Báthory's husband, who was away at war, sent tips on how to kill her victims. One charming idea was to cover them in honey so they would be bitten to death by hungry insects.

There's nothing like a good soak!

That's so sweet of him.

Kidnapped!

Báthory's victims were often teenage girls from poor families. They were lured to her castles at Csejte and Sárvár by offers of well-paid work as maids. She was helped by four servants, who also kidnapped girls from the surrounding countryside.

Now this is what I call 'blood money'.

Vlad the Impaler

Chomp!

Let off the hook

So many girls disappeared near to Báthory's castle that the local governor is said to have led a raid on the castle and arrested everyone inside. One girl was found in the hall, dead and drained of blood. Many others were found locked up in the dungeons.

She was a rich countess, so no one dared to execute Báthory. She was walled up into a room in her castle, and died there four years later.

100 years earlier, Vlad III, Prince of Wallachia (lived 1431 to 1476), got the nickname 'Impaler' after forcing a sharp stake into the bodies of 30,000 captured enemies. He was also known as Dracula, meaning the 'Son of the Dragon'. The name was later used by writer Bram Stoker for his famous vampire Dracula.

I never touched her – honest!

127

The Borgias

The Borgias were a power-mad Spanish family famous for committing murder and mayhem after moving to Rome in the mid-1400s. Their favourite trick was to invite wealthy rivals to dinner, poison them and rob them of their property. They weren't the only vicious rulers, though. In England, Tudor king Henry VIII beheaded two of his wives, while French King Louis XI wove so many plots he was known as the 'Spider King'.

Vital statistics

Name:	Borgias (Italy) or de Borjas (Spain)
Alias:	Cesare was known as 'Valentino'; Rodrigo as the 'petticoat cardinal'
In power:	1492 to 1507
Crimes:	Murder, bribery, robbery
Victims:	At least a dozen

You wouldn't want to know this: The Borgias were said to have concocted a special recipe for poisoning their rivals, a deadly blend of arsenic and phosphorus known as cantarella.

Chuckle

Cesare

Lucrezia

Guffaw

I think the wine is off, darling!

Rodrigo

Be prepared!
Always expect the very worst

Toxic times

Poisoning was all the rage in Renaissance times. There were many textbooks written describing how to create the perfect poison, and the streets of Paris were filled with professional poisoners. Toffana, a woman from Naples in Italy, even created a special poison for wives who wanted to bump off their husbands.

Ruthless rulers

Rodrigo Borgia was elected Pope Alexander VI in 1492 – after buying most of the votes. To make themselves more powerful, Rodrigo and his children accused rich nobles and church leaders of crimes then flung them in gaol or killed them. The Duke of Gandia's body was found floating in the River Tiber in Rome, probably murdered by Cesare Borgia.

Drip!

Why? Because I'm the Pope... and I say so!

Brotherly love

Most ruthless of the Borgias was Cesare, who killed anyone who got in his way, possibly even his elder brother, Giovanni. This killer streak was admired by the famous writer Niccolò Macchiavelli.

The poison beauty

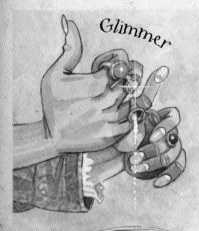

Glimmer

Rodrigo's daughter Lucrezia had a ring that was hollowed out in the middle and contained a dose of poison. Her first husband fled after her father ordered his murder, while her second was strangled by her brother Cesare's men.

The Thuggees

Throughout history, bands of vicious bandits have lain in wait to ambush travellers, such as the brigands that plagued Europe in medieval times. During the 1800s, Indian bandits known as thuggees killed countless travellers as a sacrifice to Kali, a Hindu goddess. They were so fearsome they gave the world a new word: 'thug'.

Vital statistics

Name: Thuggees
Alias: 'Stranglers' or 'Noose operators'
Active: 16th to 19th centuries
Crimes: Murder, robbery
Victims: 50,000 to 2 million

You wouldn't want to know this:

The Thuggees believed they had to kill their victims without spilling any blood, so they strangled them. This was quick and quiet and didn't alert other travellers sleeping nearby. The bodies were then buried or thrown into a nearby well.

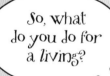

So, what do you do for a living?

Oh, you'll see...

Whistle!

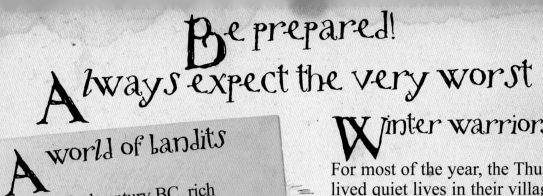

Be prepared!
Always expect the very worst

A world of bandits

- During the 2nd century BC, rich Chinese nobleman Liu Pengli led a gang of 20 to 30 outlaws who roamed the countryside murdering travellers.
- Arabian bandits preyed on travellers in the desert. They rode on camels until they got close to their victims, then switched to ponies for a burst of speed.
- During the 1250s, a group of robber barons in Germany attacked boats sailing up the Rhine river, grabbing whole ships and kidnapping those on board. They were known as the Raubritter or 'thieving knights'.

Winter warriors

For most of the year, the Thuggees lived quiet lives in their villages, causing no   suspicion. But in winter   they took to the roads.

The Thuggees' usual tactic was to join a group of travelling merchants. After winning the trust of the other merchants they robbed and killed them in a surprise night attack, choosing a place such as a river bank where it was hard for their victims to escape.

Mass murder

When the time was right, a secret signal was given, and the thuggees sprang into action. Each member of the gang had a job. Some distracted the victims or did the strangling. Others acted as lookouts or guarded the campsite so no-one escaped. The Thuggee code said the bandits couldn't kill women, blind people or carpenters, but they still murdered thousands of travellers each year.

Glark!

> Stop! I'm a whizz with a saw and hammer – and I'm blind!

No 60

Burke and Hare

In the early 19th century, two Irish labourers, Burke and Hare, came to Edinburgh, Scotland looking for work. They discovered they could make money by selling corpses to Dr Robert Knox, a surgeon who wanted to show his students the marvels of the human body. People were outraged when they heard that body snatchers were digging up fresh graves. Burke and Hare went one step further, murdering their victims to order.

It seems very fresh!

Vital Statistics

Name: William Burke (1792–1829) and William Hare (dates unknown)

Active: November 1827 to October 1828

Crimes: Murder, theft

Victims: Between 17 and 30 killed

You wouldn't want to know this:

Burke and Hare killed many of their victims by getting them drunk then smothering them – a murder method forever after known as 'burking'. This left no mark on the victims. Hare finished off one small boy by putting him over his knee and breaking his back.

Be prepared!
Always expect the very worst

Body snatchers

Gasp!

In the 1820s, Edinburgh was the place to study medicine. Doctors could cut up the corpses of criminals to show their students how a body works. But there were never enough bodies to go round. So criminals dug up dead bodies from graveyards then sold them to doctors.

Unlike other body snatchers, Burke and Hare were murderers, picking on easy targets without family or friends. Their victims included elderly pensioners, the poor and homeless, and a young boy. Hare's wife Margaret and Burke's girlfriend, Helen, lured victims off the street to Margaret's lodging house.

This way!

Bump in the night!

Another day at the office, eh?

Burke and Hare were found out when two lodgers, James and Ann Gray, heard strange noises in the night and told the police. The next day, the Grays found a victim's body under a bed. The deadly duo were arrested. Burke was tried and hanged while Hare was released for giving evidence against Burke. After his death, Burke's body was cut open in public, just like his victims. His skeleton and skin are still on display in Edinburgh.

133

Creepy Creatures

Icky insects, mythological monsters and flesh-eating beasts. Can you make it out of this section without becoming something's lunch?

№ 61

The great white shark

Sleek and streamlined, great white sharks glide with ease through the water. They live in temperate seas, from America to New Zealand. Sharks are extraordinary, ancient creatures – fishes without bones! They have tough, rubbery cartilage, instead – a survival from 150 million years ago. Today, thanks to movies and the media, almost everyone is scared of them. Sharks ARE splendid killing machines, but they rarely attack humans.

Vital statistics

Class:	*Chondrichthyes* (cartilaginous fish)
Diet:	Carnivorous (meat-eating): seals, dolphins and sea-lions
Size:	3.4–6.8 m (10.5–22.3 ft)
Weight:	3000 kg (6600 lb)
Habitat:	Temperate saltwaters
Lifespan:	Up to 100 years
Method of killing:	Biting

Yikes!

Swishhh

Great white sharks can dive 250 m (775 ft) deep. When hunting, they swim, unseen, below their prey, then ambush it by rushing towards the surface and grabbing it!

Be prepared!
Always expect the very worst

How to avoid a shark attack

- Don't swim alone. Sharks are less likely to attack groups of swimmers.

- Stay calm and quiet in the water. Sharks are curious. Noise and splashing might interest them.

- Keep away from fishing boats. They leave a trail of dead fish, blood and guts in the water, which can attract sharks.

- Get out of the water if you cut or graze yourself. A shark might detect your blood!

- If you brush up against anything rough and scaly in the water, check that you have not been bitten. Cold seas numb limbs, and some shark victims don't realise that they have been injured.

- If a shark is sighted, don't panic but DO leave the water as quickly as you can. Raise the alarm when you are safe on dry land.

- Treat all sharks – even small ones – with respect and stay out of their way.

What big teeth you have!

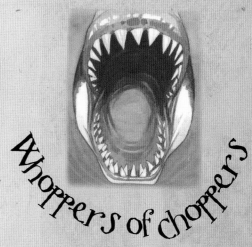

Whoppers of choppers

Sharks use electric fields (forces) in the water to help locate their prey. But sometimes these become confused and sharks eat the wrong thing, by mistake. Unlikely objects, such as car number-plates, musical instruments, and human hands and heads have been found in shark stomachs. None of these – not even human flesh – is suitable shark food. If possible, sharks will try to spit these things out.

Sharks have very sensitive noses; hitting them on the tip can deter an attack.

Sharks can sense blood and locate it from almost a mile away.

Whack!

Sniff

№62

The Brazilian wandering spider

It's silent, it scuttles, and its dull grey-brown colour makes it very hard to spot among dead leaves or in dark corners. Only its mouthparts are a bright blood red, and, if you can see them clearly, you're far too close for comfort! The Brazilian wandering spider roams town and countryside in many parts of South America, hunting for food. Its bite is deadly – perhaps the worst in the world. And its scientific name, *Phoneutria*, comes from an Ancient Greek word meaning 'murderess'.

Vital statistics

Class: *Arachnida* (spiders)
Diet: Carnivorous: flies, insects, lizards
Size: 10–12 cm (4–5 inches)
Weight: 10 mg (0.0004 oz)
Habitat: Forest floors, boxes, cupboards, car boots
Lifespan: 1–2 years
Method of killing: Venomous bite

You wouldn't want to know this:

Brazilian wandering spider bites can stop your heart beating – for ever – and cause uncontrollable bleeding.

Creep

Be prepared!
Always expect the very worst

Nasty habits

Brazilian wandering spiders:

- are very aggressive and very fast. Unlike most other spiders, who prefer to hide from humans, they will run towards people, jump up on them, and bite them.

- warn victims first. Before they attack, they raise their front legs in the air and rock from side to side.

- can bite repeatedly, every few seconds.

- use their venom to kill prey that is bigger or bulkier than themselves, such as mice and lizards. One bite contains enough venom to kill 225 mice.

- are extremely sensitive to vibrations. Because wandering spiders don't make webs, they monitor tiny movements in their surroundings to tell when possible prey – or an enemy – is approaching.

- eat each other! Like many other spiders, female Brazilian wandering spiders will kill and devour males after mating with them.

Keep calm... Don't panic!

Although Brazilian wandering spider venom is extremely poisonous, only 14 people are known to have died from it since 1926. But thousands have been bitten – and many deaths may have gone unrecorded. Sometimes the spider bites 'dry' (without venom) – very scary, but victims survive.

Often, skilled medical treatment saves lives. In 1996, an antivenin (also called anti-venom) to the venom was developed. Since then, no deaths have been reported.

Banana-box killer!

Because it likes dark, sheltered places, the Brazilian wandering spider occasionally stows away inside boxes of fruit destined for overseas supermarkets. Killer spiders have been found in European and North American stores – and have caused panic!

Shriek!

The Brazilian wandering spider's bite is extremely painful.

№ 63

The lion

'A pride of lions'. The name says it all! For centuries, lions have been honoured for their courage, strength and beauty. Prides (family groups) of lions used to live in many parts of Africa, Europe and Asia. Today, lions only survive in Africa and north-west India, where they have become great tourist attractions.

Vital statistics

Class: *Mammalia* (mammals)
Diet: Carnivorous: gazelle, buffalo, wildebeest, zebra
Size: 2.4–3.3 m (7.8–10.8 ft)
Weight: 120–225 kg (264–495 lb)
Habitat: Open woodlands, savannah (grassy plains)
Lifespan: 10–15 years
Method of killing: Biting and suffocating

Mythical monster

Lions feature in many ancient myths and legends. For example, Greek hero Heracles wore the beautiful skin of the mighty Nemean Lion. That magic monster could not be killed by human arrows, so Heracles stunned it with his war-club, then strangled it!

Be prepared!
Always expect the very worst

Man-eaters?

When most lions meet a human, they run away to hide. But a few lions develop a taste for human flesh and deliberately hunt people. This usually happens when farmers or workers move into lions' hunting territory. In one famous case, at Tsavo, Kenya, in 1898, lions killed 28 railway builders in just one year.

Expert hunters

Lions have spectacular teeth – but they don't kill by snapping or biting. Instead, they grab prey by the throat and hold it tight with their four canine teeth until it stops breathing. Then they use their back teeth like scissors for gnawing, cutting and tearing.

Killed for fun

In ancient Rome, lions were the star victims of cruel, bloodthirsty contests. They were forced to fight for their lives against gladiators armed with nets and tridents (three-pronged spears). So many lions were shipped to Rome from North Africa that they became extinct there.

Trident

Lions stalk their prey through savannah grasslands – then spring and pounce, to kill!

Chomp chomp

N⁰ 64

The saltwater crocodile

Descended from dinosaurs, saltwater crocodiles are the largest reptiles living on Earth today – and some of the most dangerous. They live in shallow waters round the coasts of south-east Asia and Australia. Like all reptiles, crocodiles are cold-blooded, and regulate their own body temperature. They bask in the sun to stay warm, or plunge into water to keep cool. They are cunning killers with no enemies, except humans.

Vital statistics

Class: *Reptilia* (reptiles)
Diet: Carnivorous: snakes, turtles, monkeys, buffalo
Size: 6–7 m (19.6–22.9 ft)
Weight: 1000–1200 kg (2200–2640 lb)
Habitat: Sea coasts, river estuaries
Lifespan: 70 years
Method of killing: Single snap of the jaws

You wouldn't want to know this:

Crocodiles can swim out to sea, where they kill sharks – and human swimmers.

Swish swoosh

Each crocodile has around 60 needle-sharp teeth, and extremely powerful jaws. When angry or alarmed, it barks, coughs and hisses.

Crunch Crunch

Mother love

A female crocodile lays around 40 eggs each year, keeping them warm in a nest of leaves and mud. After 90 days, the babies hatch. When the mother hears their cries, she uncovers the nest and carries them down to the water in her mouth. Then she watches over them until they learn to swim.

Lurking

To catch their prey, crocodiles float half-hidden in the water, waiting for prey to walk or swim by. Then they leap up, grab it and drag it underwater to eat.

Killed for fashion

In the past, crocodiles were hunted and killed so that their skin could be used to make belts and handbags. These were fashionable, costly – and an environmental disaster. Crocodiles became an endangered species. Today, crocodile skins used for fashion items come from captive animals bred on farms, not from wild crocodiles.

It's to die for!

Each crocodile skin has a unique pattern.

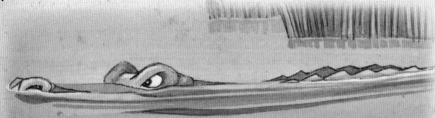

Crocodiles' brownish-green camouflage makes them very difficult to spot in muddy waters.

143

№ 65

The rat

They may be small and furry, but rats are far from cute! They spread many deadly infections – and 18 different kinds of intestinal worms! Today, as in the past, crowded, dirty cities are perfect breeding grounds for rats. Feeding on germ-filled rubbish, they spread dangerous bacteria through their faeces and urine. In the countryside, rats kill wild birds and destroy crops, trees and food stores. Rats also carry parasites – creatures that feed off other living things. There are five rats to every person in the world – and their numbers are increasing!

Vital statistics

Class: *Mammalia* (mammals)
Diet: Omnivorous (they eat everything!)
Size: 16–22 cm (6.3–8.66 in) (plus tail 20 cm/8 in)
Weight: 450–520 g (1–1.25lb)
Lifespan: 3 years
Method of killing: Spreading diseases

You wouldn't want to know this:

A female rat can give birth 7 times a year and can have up to 12 babies at a time. That means that a single female rat can have around 250 babies in its lifetime!

slurp

Be prepared!
Always expect the very worst

The plague

Arg

The deadliest disease ever spread by rats has been plague. Originating in Asia or North Africa, it killed millions of early Chinese people – and maybe many ancient Egyptians. In the 1340s and 1350s, a plague pandemic spread from Mongolia, killing 75 million people worldwide, including one-third of Europe's population. Plague struck again and again, for example in London in 1665, when 38,000 people died. The last known plague epidemic was in 1994, in Madagascar.

The flea

These microscopic parasites don't just make you itch! As fleas bite to feed on blood, they carry diseases from one living creature to another. In past epidemics, rats infested with fleas spread plague all round the world, as they stowed away on ships or cargo wagons.

The plague doctor

Plague kills most people who catch it – and its symptoms are truly terrible. Victims develop a burning fever plus buboes (huge, painful swellings). Today, plague can be cured, but in the past, all doctors could do was burst buboes with hot metal rods, and prescribe useless herbal remedies. Plague doctors tried (and failed) to protect themselves by wearing leather gloves, wax-coated robes and masks with 'beaks' full of sweet-smelling spices.

squirt!

The hippopotamus

What a surprise! Plump, waddling, vegetarian hippos are Africa's most dangerous creature! They kill hundreds of people every year, more than lions and rhinos put together. The world's third-largest living land-mammals, hippos' huge size makes them extra-dangerous if they decide to attack. They charge ferociously if their territory is invaded. On land, a charging hippo moves at 32 kph (20 mph) – much faster than any human!

Vital statistics

Class: *Mammalia* (mammals)
Diet: Herbivorous (plant-eating)
Size: 3.5–5 m (11.4–16.4 ft)
Weight: 3000–4500 kg (6600–9900 lb)
Habitat: Rivers, reed beds, grassland
Lifespan: 40 years
Method of killing: Trampling, goring, biting

You wouldn't want to know this:

Hippo teeth are 50 cm (20 in) long. An angry hippo can bite a boat full of people in half!

Male hippos defend their females and territories by challenging intruders. They gape their mouths open, 1.2 m (4 ft) wide, then crash their heads together. They also spray enemies with dung to drive them away.

Gnash

Crash

Be prepared!
Always expect the very worst

Splish Splosh

Graceful giants

On land, hippos are heavy and lumbering, but in the water they move very gracefully. Too dense (solid) to swim, they can close their ears and nostrils, and stay submerged for over 5 minutes. Their webbed toes help them to walk with ease along the river bed.

Ancient enemies

Mummies with badly broken limbs show that many ancient Egyptians were injured by hippos. Egyptians hunted hippos; they also portrayed one of their favourite goddesses, Tawaret, as a pregnant hippo.

Sweating blood?

Long ago, people thought that hippos sweated blood because their skins were covered by a red, sticky liquid. Today we know that this is a natural oil that protects a hippo's skin whenever it is out of the water.

Grunt!

Egret

Egrets

Tall white cattle egrets often follow grazing hippos, or ride on their backs. They find and eat flies, ticks and other small creatures disturbed by the hippos, or crawling on their skin.

147

No 67

The poison-dart frog

Glowing like richly coloured jewels and no bigger than a thumbnail, poison-dart frogs are miniature marvels. Almost 200 different species are found in tropical rainforests all round the world. These mild-mannered creatures kill only for food – ants, mites and flies. But the protective poison on their skin is one of the deadliest substances on Earth.

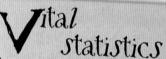

Vital statistics

Class:	*Amphibia* (amphibians)
Diet:	Insectivorous (insect-eating): ants, mites, flies
Size:	2.5–6 cm (1–2.5 in)
Weight:	2.0–6.5 g (0.07–0.23 oz)
Habitat:	Tropical rainforests
Lifespan:	4–6 years
Method of killing:	Poison

You wouldn't want to know this:

Just two micrograms (0.000002 of a gram) of dart-frog poison is enough to kill a human.

Ribbit... Ribbit...

Be prepared!
Always expect the very worst

Do not touch!

- These frogs don't use poison to kill prey or fight other frogs. Instead, they squirt it from special glands in their skin to protect themselves from predators.

- Poison-dart frogs' brilliant colouring warns other creatures not to touch or eat them. Just a single lick can kill! In spite of this, poison frogs are prey to a few snakes and large spiders, which can withstand the deadly poison.

- Some scientists think that the poisons in frogs' skin come from the foods they eat, especially the stinging ants and other insects that crawl on the rainforest floor. If captive frogs are fed non-poisonous foods, they become safe to handle.

Caring for the kids

Female frogs lay their eggs on the rainforest floor. Once the eggs have hatched into tadpoles, male frogs carry them on their backs up to tiny pools of water trapped among the plants growing on tall trees. Female frogs feed the tadpoles by laying unfertilised eggs for them to eat.

Poison darts

For thousands of years, hunters in South America, Australia and Papua New Guinea have coated darts and arrows with frog poison. When these strike prey, the poison paralyses and kills quickly. Cooking poisoned prey makes it safe to eat. The heat destroys the poison.

Croak Croak

149

No 68

The king cobra

Around 5 million snake-bites are recorded every year – and 125,000 people die from being bitten. Which snake is the deadliest? Experts do not agree – but it's probably the king cobra. It's the biggest venomous snake, the most aggressive, and one of the most feared. Unless they are promptly treated, over half its victims die. And its head can go on biting even after it has been cut off!

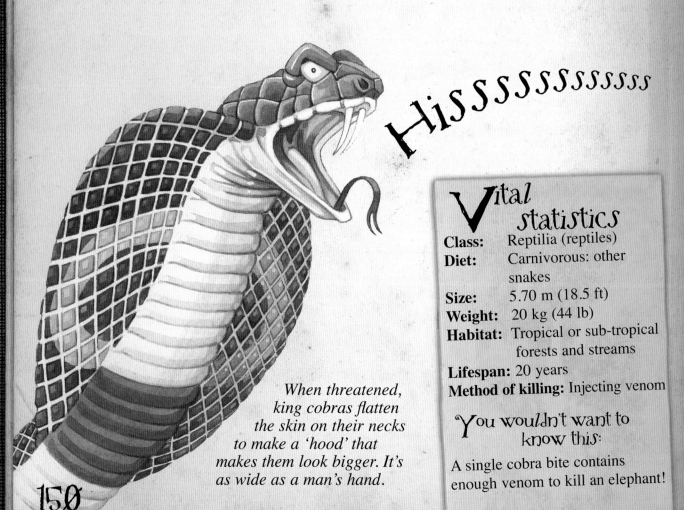

Hisssssssssss

When threatened, king cobras flatten the skin on their necks to make a 'hood' that makes them look bigger. It's as wide as a man's hand.

Vital statistics

Class: Reptilia (reptiles)
Diet: Carnivorous: other snakes
Size: 5.70 m (18.5 ft)
Weight: 20 kg (44 lb)
Habitat: Tropical or sub-tropical forests and streams
Lifespan: 20 years
Method of killing: Injecting venom

You wouldn't want to know this:

A single cobra bite contains enough venom to kill an elephant!

Be prepared!
Always expect the very worst

Keep clear

The most dangerous time to meet a king cobra is during the breeding season (early summer). Female cobras lay eggs in a nest of leaves and guard them fiercely. Male cobras attack anyone who comes near the nest, even accidentally. For the rest of the year, cobras will bite only if they are frightened, trapped or angered.

Open wide!

• King cobras have a very specialised diet – other snakes! They prefer to eat harmless species, but sometimes eat smaller cobras.

• Cobras cannot chew. Instead, their jaws open extra-wide so they can swallow their prey whole – and while it's still alive!

• The cobra's venom paralyses the swallowed creature, and starts to digest it before it reaches the cobra's stomach.

Quick killers

Cobras move very fast, on land and in water. They can also raise up the top third of their body to strike or spit venom at victims! When hunting, they use their forked tongues to flick a prey's scent into their mouths, where it is recognised by a special sensor.

Cobras' excellent eyesight means that they can spot creatures up to 100 m (330 ft) away. At night, they detect their prey's movements by sensing minute changes of temperature.

Hissss   Aargh!

151

Nº 69

The Australian box jellyfish

Transparent, pale blue and almost invisible, Australian box jellyfish bring death on every summer tide. From November to May, colonies of these graceful, grapefruit-sized, jelly killers float in the warm waters of the Pacific Ocean, coming close to the shore – and to surfers' beaches. A few victims have survived an attack by box jellyfish stinging tentacles – but say that the pain was so bad that they would rather have died!

Ssswish

Gulp!

Box jellyfish use their tentacles to catch fish

Vital statistics

Class: *Cubozoa* (box-shaped invertebrates)
Diet: Carnivorous: small fish, worms, shrimp
Size: 25 cm (10 in) bell, plus 3 m (9.8 ft) tentacles
Weight: 2 kg (4.4 lb)
Habitat: Warm Pacific waters
Lifespan: 3–6 months
Method of killing: Injects venom

You wouldn't want to know this:

The box jellyfish makes no warning noise and gives no danger signal. It's a silent, stealthy killer!

Be prepared!
Always expect the very worst

Jet-propelled!

With no arms and legs to carry them, how do box jellyfish move along? By jet propulsion! Box jellyfish shoot through the sea by squeezing their bells (bodies) into a ball, pushing the water out behind them. Travelling this way, they move at around 8 km (5 miles) per hour – as fast as an Olympic swimmer!

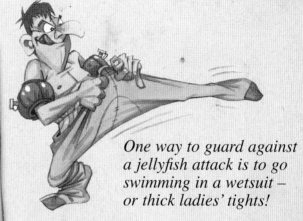

One way to guard against a jellyfish attack is to go swimming in a wetsuit – or thick ladies' tights!

Stinging cells

- The long, trailing tentacles of box jellyfish are covered with microscopic nematocysts (stinging cells). Scientists think there are around 3 million of them on every square centimetre of tentacle.

- Each stinging cell contains a barb (spike) as well as deadly venom. If a stinging cell touches a fish – or a human – it explodes, firing its barb and venom into the skin of its prey.

- A box jellyfish sting causes humans instant pain, followed by cramp, vomiting, frothing at the mouth, loss of speech, paralysis – and death. Splashing vinegar onto the sting neutralises the venom, but victims also need rapid treatment with antivenin to fight the poison.

How do jellyfish feed?

As it floats along, the box jellyfish is also busy hunting. Its trailing tentacles are designed to trap small fish or shrimp swimming nearby. Once prey is caught, flaps at the bottom of the jellyfish's bell waft it towards a tube tipped with a four-cornered mouth. The tube sucks up the prey and passes it into the jellyfish's stomach.

No 70
The mosquito

They're almost weightless and incredibly fragile, but Anopheles mosquitoes cause more human deaths than any other creature. They spread a dangerous disease called malaria to between 300 and 500 million people every year, mostly in Africa. More than 2 million die. Children, pregnant women, old people and the sick are most at risk.

Vital statistics

Class: *Insecta* (Insects)
Diet: Carnivorous: blood
Size: 0.3–2 cm (0.012–0.78 in)
Weight: 2.5 mg (0.00009 oz)
Habitat: Warm, wet regions, mostly Africa.
Lifespan: 2 weeks – 6 months
Method of killing: Spreading disease

You wouldn't want to know this:

Only females are killers! A microscopic parasite lives in the female mosquito's stomach. When she bites a human and drinks the blood, she injects the parasite into them. It multiplies, and causes malaria.

BUZZZZzz

Slurp

Be prepared!
Always expect the very worst

Please buzz off!

Finding a victim

A female mosquito has no nose. But she has sensors that can detect people moving, sweating or breathing out carbon dioxide. Her tiny body also contains chemicals that sense other human smells, and lead her towards them.

How to combat a mosquito attack

Without protection, a person in a mosquito-ridden area can be bitten between 50 and 100 times in one night! The best ways to avoid bites are to:

- sleep inside a mosquito net (a tent made of netting).

- keep your skin covered.

- use anti-insect spray.

- coat walls (where mosquitoes rest) with insect-killer.

- keep fires burning close by — mosquitos don't like smoke.

Pssssst

Life-cycle of a mosquito

After mating and feeding on blood, the female mosquito lays about 200 eggs in shallow water. These hatch into hungry larvae, eating tiny scraps of dead animals and growing all the time. At last, the larvae pupate (wrap themselves in a cocoon). Inside, they transform themselves into adult insects, with wings and six legs.

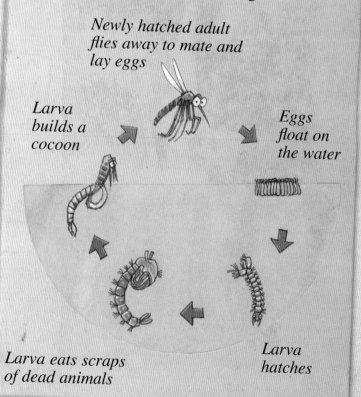

Newly hatched adult flies away to mate and lay eggs

Larva builds a cocoon

Eggs float on the water

Larva eats scraps of dead animals

Larva hatches

Nº 71

Masiakasaurus

A bipedal dinosaur with a long neck and tail, Masiakasaurus had one extraordinary feature – its terrifying teeth. Its long, sharp front teeth pointed forward, which is rare for predatory dinosaurs. Its vicious lower front teeth were almost horizontal, and would have been ideal for spearing prey. Its blade-like back teeth cut and ripped its victim's flesh into tasty, bite-sized chunks.

Vital statistics

Name:	Masiakasaurus (mah-shee-ah-kah-SORE-us)
Meaning:	Vicious lizard
Length:	Up to 2 m (6 ft)
Weight:	35 kg (77 lb)
Diet:	Carnivorous
Time span:	84-71 mya
Period:	Late Cretaceous
Found:	Madagascar

You wouldn't want to know this:

A piece of fossilised dinosaur dung is called a coprolite and it can tell us how, who and what the dinosaur ate!

Tremble!

Masiakasaurus' diet consisted of fish, lizards and other, smaller dinosaurs.

Be prepared!
Always expect the very worst

Dinosaur teeth

Scientists studying a dinosaur's fossilised teeth can discover what it ate, how it got the food, and whether it chewed, crushed, or just swallowed it whole! Teeth are harder than bone and fossilise more easily. This is how we know that some dinosaurs existed even though only their teeth remain.

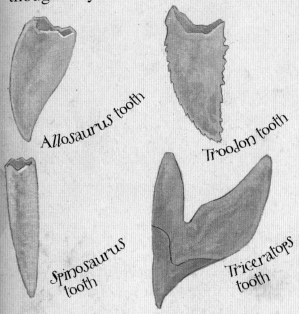

Allosaurus tooth

Troodon tooth

Spinosaurus tooth

Triceratops tooth

Fierce carnivores like Allosaurus and Tyrannosaurus rex had sharp, pointed teeth for tearing flesh. If the dinosaur had powerful jaws, their teeth would be used for crushing their victim's bones. Triceratops used its toothless beak to gather up vegetation and its flat cheek teeth to chew tough plant material. Troodon snarled through serrated teeth, ideal for cutting through tough meat and sinews.

Gnashers!

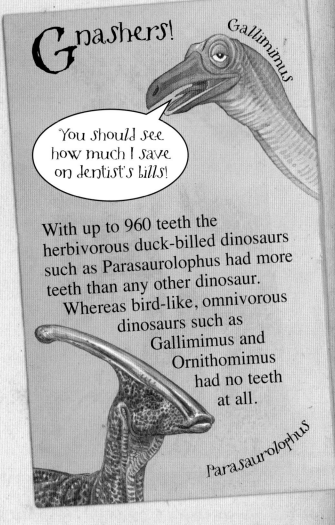

Gallimimus

You should see how much I save on dentist's bills!

With up to 960 teeth the herbivorous duck-billed dinosaurs such as Parasaurolophus had more teeth than any other dinosaur. Whereas bird-like, omnivorous dinosaurs such as Gallimimus and Ornithomimus had no teeth at all.

Parasaurolophus

Mashed to a pulp

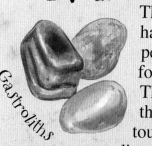

Gastroliths

The large herbivores had spoon-shaped or peg-like teeth designed for stripping plants. They didn't chew their food. Instead, the tough plant material was digested inside their huge guts. Many plant-eating dinosaurs swallowed gastroliths, or 'stomach stones', that helped to grind up the leaves and twigs.

No 72

Eocarcharia dinops

The fierce-eyed dinosaur Eocarcharia dinops used its huge and immensely hard brow-bone to butt rival males and attract potential mates. Its 7.6 cm (3 inch) long teeth were blade-shaped, just ideal for disabling live dinosaurs and severing their body parts! The top predator of its day, Eocarcharia's chief prey was the long-necked plant-eater, Nigersaurus.

Vital statistics

Name:	Eocarcharia (EE-oh-kahr-kar-ee-uh)
Meaning:	Dawn shark
Length:	6-8 m (19-26 ft)
Weight:	Up to1,600 kg (1.6 tonnes)
Diet:	Carnivorous
Time span:	112-99.6 mya
Period:	Cretaceous
Found:	Niger, North Africa

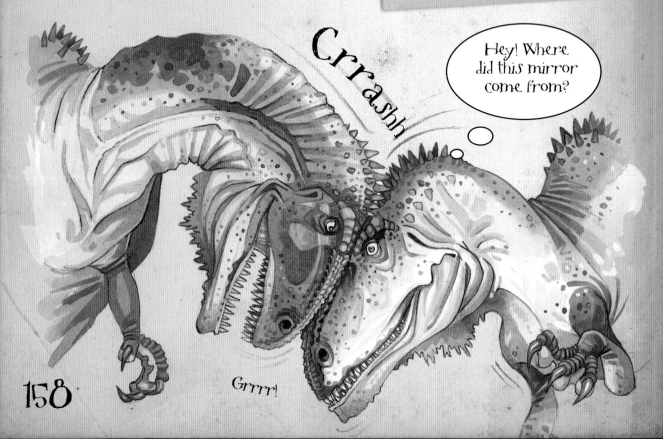

Crrashh

Hey! Where did this mirror come from?

Grrrr!

Granddaddy dinosaur

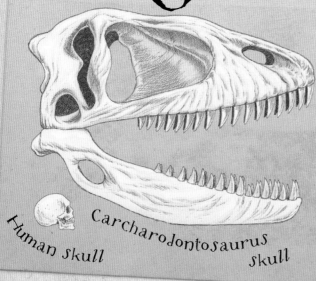

Carcharodontosaurus skull

Human skull

Over a long period of time, Eocarcharia dinops evolved into an even larger predator, Carcharodontosaurus. Carcharodontosaurus was a monstrous carnivore with a heavy-boned bulky body, and a massive tail. It grew up to 14 m (46 ft) long and weighed up to 15,000 kg (15 tonnes). When it reached full size its skull was as big as a fully-formed human!

Nigersaurus had a mouth shaped like the end of a vacuum cleaner. It ate vegetation from the ground like a modern cow.

Eocarcharia would have been too slow to run down most other dinosaurs. However, this deadly killer may have lain in wait and pounced on other dinosaurs when they weren't expecting it.

Nigersaurus

Munch!

Smack!

My mother always told me not to eat fast food!

№ 73

Triceratops

Although deceptively peaceful, Triceratops' long horns and strong body would have made it a formidable opponent for even an aggressive carnivore like Tyrannosaurus rex. Triceratops' head alone weighed a massive 455 kg (1,000 lb). When it charged to attack, Triceratops' 1.2 m (4 ft) long horns were capable of digging into the predator's flesh, even penetrating its heart. The solid bone attached to its skull shielded Triceratops' soft body from attack.

Vital statistics

Name:	Triceratops (tri-SERRA-tops)
Meaning:	Three-horned face
Length:	Up to 9 m (29 ft)
Weight:	6-12 tonnes
Diet:	Herbivorous
Time span:	67-65 mya
Period:	Late Cretaceous
Found:	USA

Grrrr!

Despite its small brain Triceratops was one of the most successful dinosaurs of the late Cretaceous Period. It was one of the last dinosaurs to have existed.

I'm a survivor! I put it down to the fruit and veg... oh, and the horns!

Turning heads

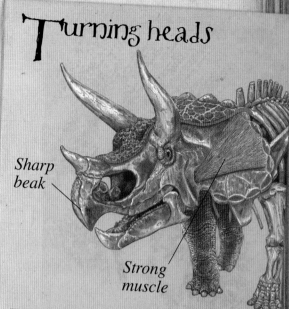

Sharp beak

Strong muscle

Horrible horns

Triceratops probably lived in small groups. The male with the largest and sharpest horns would be capable not just of defending its territory, but also of beating a rival male when it was time to mate.

Triceratops had a special joint at the base of its skull, allowing it to move its head almost 360 degrees. In a fraction of a second it could position its head, ready to face a threatening predator.

Crrunch

Quetzalcoatlus

Quetzalcoatlus was one of the largest flying creatures to ever exist. This truly terrifying creature existed during the Cretaceous Period and, like the dinosaurs, was a reptile.

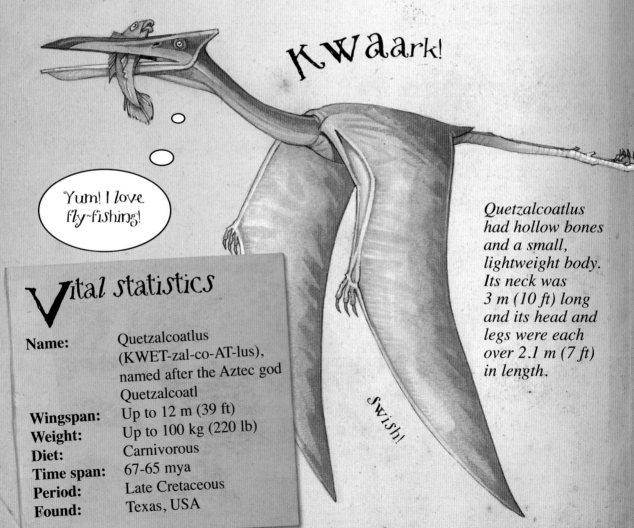

KWaark!

Yum! I love fly-fishing!

Quetzalcoatlus had hollow bones and a small, lightweight body. Its neck was 3 m (10 ft) long and its head and legs were each over 2.1 m (7 ft) in length.

Swish!

Vital statistics

Name:	Quetzalcoatlus (KWET-zal-co-AT-lus), named after the Aztec god Quetzalcoatl
Wingspan:	Up to 12 m (39 ft)
Weight:	Up to 100 kg (220 lb)
Diet:	Carnivorous
Time span:	67-65 mya
Period:	Late Cretaceous
Found:	Texas, USA

Be prepared!
Always expect the very worst

Eagle-eyed

Whoosh!

The wings of Quetzalcoatlus were covered by a thin, leathery layer that stretched between its body, the top of its legs and its long fourth fingers. Claws protruded from the other fingers. It was able to soar vast distances and it had good eyesight, which it used to spot prey from the air. A flock of these incredible animals must have been an absolutely awesome sight!

Corpse-eater

Quetzalcoatlus lived inland, near fresh-water lakes. It hunted fish by gliding over water using its long, toothless jaws to scoop up and filter its prey. Quetzalcoatlus was also a gruesome scavenger, walking on all fours in order to feed on the bodies of dead dinosaurs.

Chomp!

What can I say? He had a *lot of guts!*

Although it wasn't technically a dinosaur itself, Quetzalcoatlus was a distant cousin to the dinosaurs. This huge flying reptile is included in this book because it was an incredibly scary creature.

№ 75

Troodon

What made Troodon more frightening than other, larger, carnivorous dinosaurs, was its big brain and the ability to hunt at night, sometimes in packs. A group of hungry Troodon would be absolutely terrifying, eating just about anything they could slash and tear apart with their sharp teeth and huge, sickle-shaped toe claws.

Raaar!

Troodon

Saurornithoides

Vital statistics

Name:	Troodon (TROH-oh-don)
Meaning:	Wounding tooth
Length:	Up to 2 m (6.5 ft)
Weight:	50 kg (110 lb)
Diet:	Carnivorous
Time span:	74-65 mya
Period:	Late Cretaceous
Found:	USA

Be prepared!
Always expect the very worst

Brain box

An animal's intelligence is measured by EQ (encephalisation quotient). This is the size of the brain compared to the size of the body. The more of the body is taken up by the brain, the more intelligent the animal.

Massospondylus, an early herbivore, had a very low EQ and was one of the least intelligent dinosaurs. Whereas Troodon had one of the largest brains compared to the size of its body, and a higher EQ than any other dinosaur.

Massospondylus

Remember, boys – no growling or you'll give us away!

Stalk!

Egg laying

Female Troodons usually produced two eggs, which they incubated in earth nests. Like chickens, they often sat on the eggs, using their own body heat to warm them.

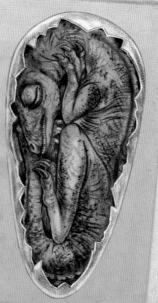

Night stalker

Troodon was only about the size of a human, so it was lightweight and able to run fast. A good sense of hearing and large, slightly forward-facing eyes allowed Troodon to pursue its prey in the dark.

165

Kronosaurus

An extremely scary marine reptile, Kronosaurus lived during the age of the dinosaurs. Kronosaurus was about the same size as a present-day sperm whale. Kronosaurus' sheer bulk meant it could eat almost any creature that swam past, including other marine reptiles, giant squid, large fish and probably the occasional unlucky dinosaur that passed too close to the shore.

Vital statistics

Name:	Kronosaurus (crow-no-SORE-us)
Meaning:	Titan lizard
Length:	Up to 12.5 m (41 ft)
Weight:	Up to 22 tonnes
Diet:	Carnivorous
Time span:	144-199 mya
Period:	Early Cretaceous
Found:	Australia

You wouldn't want to know this:

Kronosaurus is named after Kronos, the Greek god of time, who was so awful that he ate his own children.

Eeeeek!

And you just wanted to get your feet wet …

Sploosh!

Be prepared!
Always expect the very worst

Flipping fast

Kronosaurus' smooth body was driven through the water by four of the most powerful flippers ever developed by a marine animal. Capable of bursts of incredible speed, few creatures could escape it.

Big head!

This formidable predator had an enormous head, up to one third of the length of its body. Its strong jaws and 15 cm (6 inch) long teeth enabled it to crush the shells of giant turtles and large ammonites.

Giant squid

Car-sized turtle

Archelon was a huge turtle over 3.6 m (12 ft) long. A carnivore, Archelon probably ate jellyfish. When threatened by Kronosaurus it would have pulled its strong flippers into its thick protective shell.

Archelon

Nº 77

Allosaurus

The most successful carnivorous dinosaur of its time, Allosaurus was a fearsome, fast and agile hunter. Allosaurus had a short neck, a long tail and a massive skull with two blunt horns. Its jaws were lined with curved, dagger-like teeth, which had serrated edges like the blade of a steak knife. Allosaurus had strong talon-like claws on its hands and feet, enabling it to hold down and tear at its prey, which included large herbivorous dinosaurs such as Camptosaurus and Stegosaurus.

Well 'allo there!

Vital statistics

Name:	Allosaurus (AL-oh-saw-russ)
Meaning:	Other lizard
Length:	Up to 12 m (39 ft)
Weight:	Up to 4.5 tonnes
Diet:	Carnivorous
Time span:	153-135 mya
Period:	Late Jurassic
Found:	Tanzania and USA

Be prepared!
Always expect the very worst

Childcare

Fossil evidence suggests that Allosaurus may have protected its children. It may have dragged dead carcasses back to its lair, feeding the young until they were fully grown, fending off any scavengers that might attack.

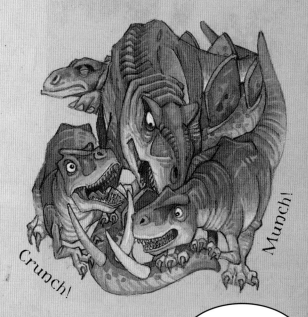

Crunch!

Munch!

Vicious hunter

Allosaurus used its huge tail to help trap prey, and could tear the flesh off it whilst it was still alive! When the opportunity arose Allosaurus would scavenge for food, not only eating carcasses but also driving away smaller dinosaurs from their own kills.

Grrrr!

Growl!

Apatosaurus

Chomp!

Get off me, you big bullies!

Size doesn't matter

Even enormous dinosaurs like Apatosaurus and Diplodocus were not safe from attack. Hunting groups of Allosaurus would have brought down the weakest members picked from a herd of these monster herbivores.

No 73

Megaraptor

The fierce, bird-like dinosaur Megaraptor was incredibly deadly. This extreme predator had a lethal 35 cm (14 inch) long, sickle-shaped claw on each foot. Megaraptor had a curved neck and a huge head. Its immensely powerful jaws were armed with very sharp, serrated teeth. It was an intelligent dinosaur, so if Megaraptor hunted in packs it could probably kill any prey it wanted.

Despite its name, Megaraptor was not a raptor. Raptors were small to medium-sized carnivorous dinosaurs with large brains, two legs and hands that could grasp. You can find more information about these vicious dinosaurs on the opposite page.

Rraaaawwr!

Vital statistics

Name:	Megaraptor (meg-a-RAP-tor)
Meaning:	Huge robber
Length:	6-8 m (up to 26 ft)
Diet:	Carnivorous
Time span:	90-84 mya
Period:	Late Cretaceous
Found:	South America

Terrible claw

The raptor Deinonychus more than lived up to its name 'Terrible Claw'.

After chasing a similar-sized dinosaur like Hypsilophodon, Deinonychus overpowered its prey.

It tore open Hypsilophodon's body with its terrifying sharp-clawed fingers and sickle-like talons.

Speed kills

Zoom!

Utahraptor was one of the largest raptors that ever lived. Reaching speeds of up to 100 kph (62 mph), these large-eyed raptors could spot and run down any prey they chose. As pack hunters, Utahraptors may have used one member as bait while the others caught and killed prey up to twice their size.

Tenontosaurus

Yum! Now this is what I call fresh meat!

Chew!

Deinonychus

Working together, a group of Deinonychus, 3 m (9.9 ft) long raptors, could bring down a massive 6.5 m (21 ft) long Tenontosaurus.

Snarl!

№ 79

Tyrannosaurus rex

Tyrannosaurus rex certainly was a fearsome dinosaur. This awesome carnivore had an enormous skull with massive 1.2 m (4 ft) long, muscular jaws packed with large, pointed teeth. It could run as fast as 24 kph (15 mph).

Tyrannosaurus rex had between 50 and 60 cone-shaped, saw-edged teeth for tearing flesh and crushing bones. They varied in size but the largest teeth were huge, up to 33 cm (13 inches) long including the root. Like most dinosaurs, Tyrannosaurus rex's teeth were replaceable. As teeth were lost or broken from fighting or eating, new teeth grew to replace them.

Vital statistics

Name: Tyrannosaurus rex (tie-RAN-oh-sore-us rex)
Meaning: Tyrant lizard king
Length: Up to 13 m (42.6 ft)
Weight: 5-7 tonnes
Diet: Carnivorous
Time span: 67-65 mya
Period: Late Cretaceous
Found: USA, Canada, East Asia

You wouldn't want to know this:

Tyrannosarus rex had an enormous, one metre wide open mouth which could rip apart a carcass with frightening ease.
It could eat up to 230 kg (507 lb) of meat and bones in one bite!

Roar!

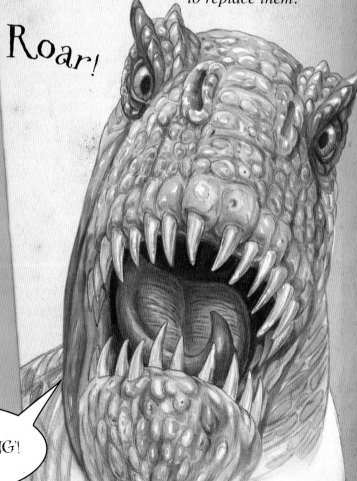

That's right – 'tyrant lizard KING'! Don't forget it!

Be prepared!
Always expect the very worst

Getting going

(a)

Tyrannosaurus probably rested on its stomach. However, because of its weight, getting up would have been a problem.

(b)

Tyrannosaurus may have used its small front legs for balance as it started to rise.

(c)

When its back legs were nearly straight it could throw its head back, using the momentum to lift itself off the ground.

(d)

Once fully upright Tyrannosaurus would be ready to set out in search of food.

Albertosaurus

Tyrannosaurus rex

Crunch!

Daspletosaurus

Chomp!

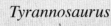
Munch!

What a pong!

Although Tyrannosaurus rex hunted alone, a heightened sense of smell helped it find dead flesh when there was little live meat around. Tyrannosaurus dismembered and ate the dead animal quickly: the stench of a rotting carcass would have attracted scavengers from far off. Albertosaurus and Daspletosaurus, which were both relatives of Tyrannosaurus, would have joined in the feast.

173

No 80

Spinosaurus

The largest carnivorous dinosaur that we know of was the extremely scary Spinosaurus, which could grow up to an amazing 18 m long!
This merciless dinosaur would attack and eat smaller prey of any kind, as well as scavenging from dead dinosaurs.
Like a present-day crocodile, its long narrow snout contained jaws filled with short, sharp, straight teeth and its nostrils faced upwards.
This meant that it was probably able to hunt sharks and other fish in nearby mangrove swamps.

Vital statistics

Name:	Spinosaurus (SPINE-oh-SORE-us)
Meaning:	Thorn lizard
Length:	Up to 18 m (59 ft)
Weight:	4-8 tonnes
Diet:	Carnivorous
Time span:	95-70 mya
Period:	Late Cretaceous
Found:	Egypt, Morocco

Eeek!

Be prepared!
Always expect the very worst

Dimetrodon

Dimetrodon, a fierce carnivore, lived nearly 200 million years before Spinosaurus. It too had a sail along its back. Dimetrodon was an early reptile, an ancestor to the mammals, called a pelycosaur.

Hot or cold?

The distinctive spines of the Spinosaurus grew up to 2 m (6.5 ft) long, with skin stretching between them like a sail. This sail made Spinosaurus appear larger and even more threatening to any rivals. Many scientists think that Spinosaurus also used its sail to manage its body temperature, rather like a radiator.

Sail

Spines

Growl!

Little and large

Spinosaurus probably had the longest head of any known carnivorous dinosaur! Its mouth was nearly 2 m (6.5 ft) long. At the other end of the scale we have the Microraptor, which is the tiniest dinosaur ever discovered. At only 60 cm (2 ft) long, this bizarre dinosaur had two pairs of primitive wings – one set on its forearms and the other on its hind legs. The swift-moving Microraptor lived in trees and fed on insects.

I'd better buzz off!

Microraptor

Raaar!

No 81
Thunderbird

Listen! Can you hear him? Thunderbird is coming! Swooping down from his home in the sky, he brings wild winds in his wings. Thunderclaps shake the world whenever he flaps his feathers. When he blinks, lightning flashes from his eyes. Don't anger him or he'll send floods and storms to destroy you!

Whoosh!

Whoosh!

Vital statistics

Name: Thunderbird
Appearance: Multicoloured eagle
Size: Wingspan wide as two canoes
Armed with: Beak, horns, talons
Home: North America
Powers: Brings violent storms

You wouldn't want to know this:
Thunderbird carries deadly snakes – like forked lightning – under his wings.

Today's weather forecast is mild, with showers of DEATH and DESTRUCTION!

Crackle!

Be prepared!
Always expect the very worst

Thunderbird vs. whale

Once, a monster whale devoured all the fish in the sea. Everyone was starving! Thunderbird attacked the whale, and they fought a terrible battle. Thunderbird won, and hurled the whale deep down into the ocean (where it still lives). Or else, some say, he carried it up to his lair and ate it!

Sign of strength

With its mighty wings spread wide, a carved Thunderbird keeps watch at the top of a tall totem pole in Canada. He's a sign of strength, an honoured ancestor, and a guardian.

Thunderbird lives among the clouds, at the top of a holy mountain.

Revenge of the Roc

Look out! Here it comes: the Roc, another giant bird, from Asia. It carries its lunch – an elephant! – and is ready to sink ships by dropping huge boulders onto them!

squawk!

Help! Put me down!

177

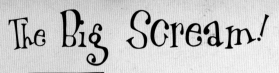

Mermaid

Pretty but deadly, mermaids kill by mistake. They sit smiling sweetly on jagged rocks, beckoning sailors to jump from passing ships to join them. Or they clasp sailors in their loving arms and take them to mermaid palaces underwater. Either way, the sailors drown, of course…

Vital statistics

Name: Mermaid
Appearance: Half woman, half fish
Size: Up to 61 metres (200 feet) long
Armed with: Sweet voice, long hair (sometimes green!), pretty face
Home: Rocky shores
Powers: Fatal charm

You wouldn't want to know this:

Seeing a mermaid brings dreadful disaster.

There are mermen, too, but they don't wreck ships or kill sailors.

I hope they stick around a bit longer this time!

Be prepared!
Always expect the very worst

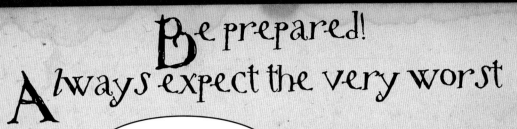

You seem to have made a mer~stake!

Mistaken identity

This gentle sea-creature has an appealing face and a friendly, inquisitive nature. But no, it's not a mermaid, as past sailors supposed. It's a real-life sea-cow, or manatee!

Spirit of the waters

You may see Mami Wata gliding through West African waves, or admiring her face in a mirror. But whenever you meet her, beware! Her brilliant jewellery can blind you!

Sinister singers

Sirens were monstrous sisters (half bird, half girl) who made the best music in the world. But hearing their songs lured sailors onto dangerous rocks – and then the Sirens devoured them!

Tra~la~la!

Sparkle!

The Sirens sang in Ancient Greece, over two thousand years ago.

№83

Cyclops

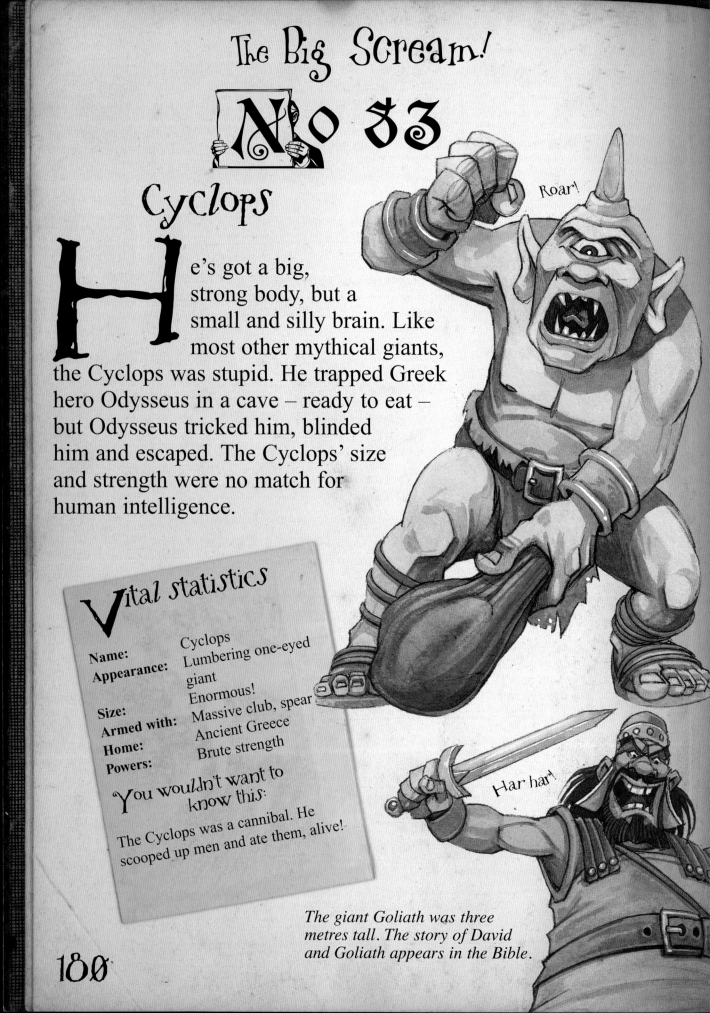

He's got a big, strong body, but a small and silly brain. Like most other mythical giants, the Cyclops was stupid. He trapped Greek hero Odysseus in a cave – ready to eat – but Odysseus tricked him, blinded him and escaped. The Cyclops' size and strength were no match for human intelligence.

Roar!

Vital statistics

Name: Cyclops
Appearance: Lumbering one-eyed giant
Size: Enormous!
Armed with: Massive club, spear
Home: Ancient Greece
Powers: Brute strength

You wouldn't want to know this:

The Cyclops was a cannibal. He scooped up men and ate them, alive!

Har har!

The giant Goliath was three metres tall. The story of David and Goliath appears in the Bible.

Be prepared!
Always expect the very worst

I think I'll buy myself a big, sharp axe...

Gleam!

Sniff, sniff, sniff!

In the fairytale, Young Jack climbed a tall beanstalk to reach a giant's castle. But the giant was greedy, ravenously hungry, and had a very keen sense of smell! How did Jack escape? The giant's wife took pity on him, and helped him.

Record breaker

There are giants in the real world, as well as in myths and fairytales. Sultan Kosen (born 1982), a farmer from Turkey, holds the world record as today's tallest man.

Sultan Kosen (on the right) is 2.47 m (8 ft 1 in) tall.

Giant-killer

For forty days, the giant warrior Goliath challenged the Israelites. But no-one dared fight him – except for young David. He killed Goliath with just one pebble, hurled from a sling.

Take this!

Nº 54

Kraken

eep in the ocean lurks a mighty monster: Kraken. Big as an island! Looks like a giant squid! Its huge bulging body makes fearsome whirlpools as it swims along, and its waving tentacles can pull the largest ships to the bottom of the sea.

Vital statistics

Name:	Kraken
Appearance:	Like a giant squid
Size:	20 metres or more
Armed with:	Tentacles, sharp beak
Home:	Atlantic and Arctic Oceans
Powers:	Wrecks ships, drowns sailors

You wouldn't want to know this:

Kraken swallows small fish and belches them up, before eating the bigger fish that come to feast on the vomit. Yuk!

Help! The Kraken's crackin' the ship!

Splash!

Be prepared!
Always expect the very worst

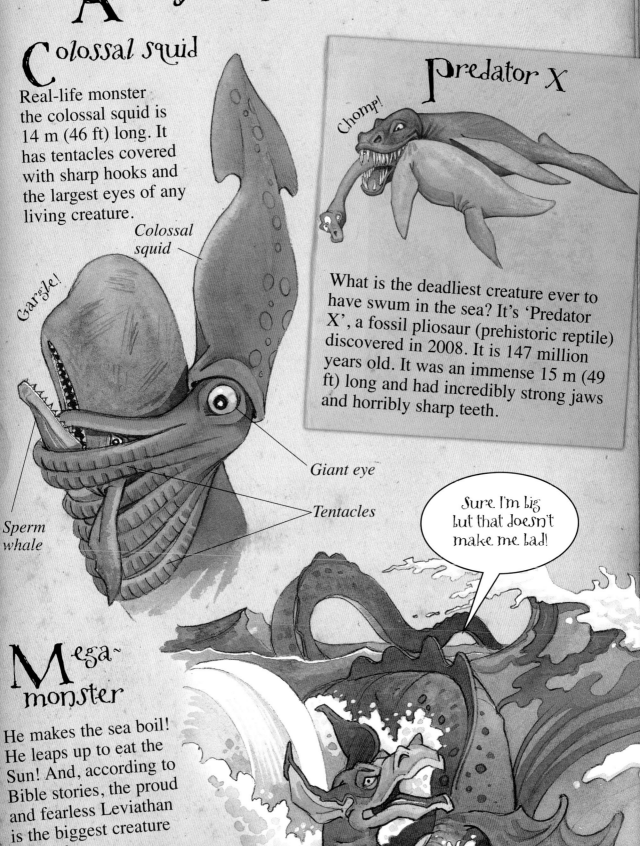

Colossal squid

Real-life monster the colossal squid is 14 m (46 ft) long. It has tentacles covered with sharp hooks and the largest eyes of any living creature.

Colossal squid

Gargle!

Giant eye

Tentacles

Sperm whale

Predator X

Chomp!

What is the deadliest creature ever to have swum in the sea? It's 'Predator X', a fossil pliosaur (prehistoric reptile) discovered in 2008. It is 147 million years old. It was an immense 15 m (49 ft) long and had incredibly strong jaws and horribly sharp teeth.

Sure I'm big but that doesn't make me bad!

Mega-monster

He makes the sea boil! He leaps up to eat the Sun! And, according to Bible stories, the proud and fearless Leviathan is the biggest creature on Earth.

Nº 35

The Minotaur

The Minotaur had the mind of a man trapped inside the lumbering body of a bull. He was tragic and terrible, fierce and furious, neither man nor beast, but a mixture of both. His mother's husband, King Minos of Crete, had a special maze built to hide him, called the Labyrinth.

Snort!

Bull's head and horns

You won't like me when I'm angry... or annoyed... or mildly peeved!

Vital statistics

Name: Minotaur
Appearance: Part human, part bull
Size: Like a mighty man
Armed with: Superhuman strength
Home: Crete, a Greek island
Powers: Preyed on human flesh

You wouldn't want to know this:

Seven girls and seven boys were fed to the Minotaur every year.

Man's body

Be prepared!
Always expect the very worst

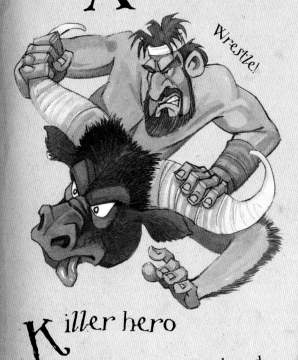

Wrestle!

Fair face, foul heart

Like the Minotaur, the Manticore was a hybrid (a mixture of more than one animal). It had a human head, a lion's body and a poisonous scorpion's tail. It looked good, but was deadly.

Grrr!

The Manticore was a symbol of the bad side of human nature.

Killer hero

Not only the son of a Greek god but a prince, athlete and dancer to boot, Theseus entered the Labyrinth, trailing thread behind him. He killed the Minotaur, then followed the thread out again. He was the only man ever to leave the Labyrinth alive.

The dance of death

Seize a fierce bull by the horns, then somersault over its back. Landed safely? You're lucky! Gored to death? You're a human sacrifice to the Greek gods!

Painting of bull-dancers from King Minos' palace, made around 2000 BC.

No 86

The Yeti

A joke, a mystery, a hoax, a prehistoric human or an undiscovered species of ape? For over 100 years, people have puzzled about the Yeti. Some say it is a real creature that leaves tracks on snowy mountains. Others say that it simply does not exist!

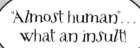

'Almost human'... what an insult!

Flat face, almost human

Huge bear-like chest

Long, strong arms

Thick, shaggy hair

Giant feet

Vital statistics

Name: Yeti (Man-Bear)

Appearance: Very hairy, huge feet, sharp claws

Size: Up to 3 metres (nearly 10 feet) tall

Armed with: Stealth and strength

Home: Himalaya Mountains in Tibet, China, India

Powers: Rides horses and yaks, survives in snowy wilderness

You wouldn't want to know this:

Some reports say that Yetis kidnap humans and keep them as pets.

186

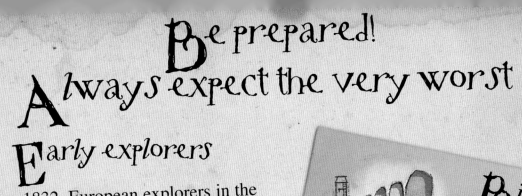

Be prepared!
Always expect the very worst

Early explorers

Since 1832, European explorers in the Himalayan mountain range of Asia have reported sightings of a strange wild creature that left mysterious tracks in the snow.

Bigfoot

What leaves footprints over 60 cm (2 ft) long and 20 cm (8 inches) wide? 'Bigfoot': a monster like the Yeti that is said to live in the North-West of North America.

Several people claim to have seen Bigfoot. Film footage showing a huge, hairy creature, almost 3 m (10 ft) tall, was recorded in California in 1967. But who knows whether the pictures were fake or real?

No way am I going back up there!

lurk!

At last I can sleep safe at night!

Under the microscope

Imagine the excitement when explorers found clumps of 'Yeti' hair in a Tibetan monastery! But in 2008, scientists proved that the hair came from a goral. A goral is a Himalayan animal rather like a goat. What a disappointment!

187

No 89

Werewolf

What would it be like to change shape, to be transformed into an animal? That's what happens to werewolves, mostly at full moon. One minute, they're a normal person, the next, they have hairy skin, huge fangs, slavering jaws – and a hunger for dead bodies!

Vital statistics

Name: Werewolf
Appearance: Wolf standing upright like a human
Size: Large, lean, hungry wolf
Armed with: Sharp fangs and strong jaws
Home: Europe and North America
Powers: Kills; eats corpses; steals children

You wouldn't want to know this:

Women werewolves have poisonous claws – and can kill children just by looking at them!

Howwwl! Grrrrr! Snarrrl!

It is said that a werewolf can only be killed by a silver bullet.

Be prepared!
Always expect the very worst

Spot a werewolf: handy checklist

- Curved fingernails
- Ears low on head
- Eyebrows meet over the nose
- Bristles under the tongue

Hmm, should I see a doctor or eat one?

How to become a werewolf

- Be bitten by a werewolf
- Rub body with magic ointment
- Drink special potion
- Be cursed by holy person
- Drink water from werewolf's footprint
- Put on wolfskin belt
- Sleep outside, under a full moon

I always seem to get peckish at full moon!

Monster baby?

Strange creatures with snarling faces and wolf-like fangs appear in myths from many different lands. Most famous are 'were-jaguars' – half human, half jaguar – from the Olmec civilisation of Central America. They loved rain, not blood!

Split head

Snarling mouth

Hands like paws

Olmec stone carving of were-jaguar made around 1000 BC.

Wolf warriors

In Viking times (around AD 800–1100) fighting men joined elite teams of wolf-warriors, the Ulfhednar. They dressed in wolf-skins, making them look like werewolves, and worked themselves into a savage killing frenzy before battle.

Aroooooo!

Medusa the Gorgon

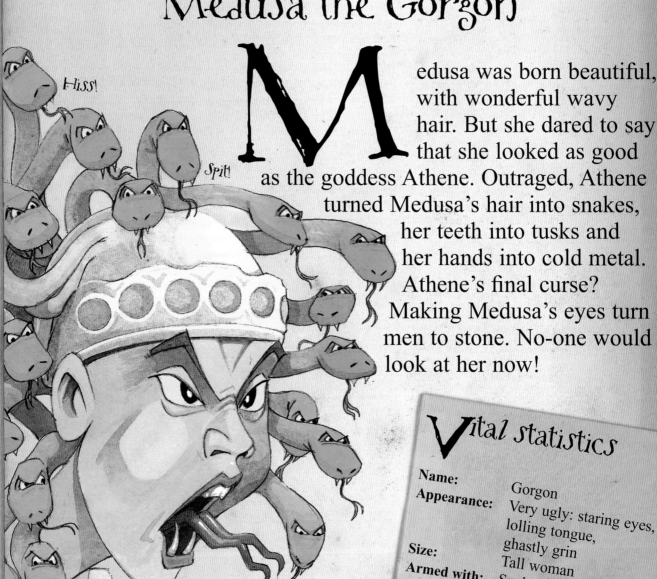

Medusa was born beautiful, with wonderful wavy hair. But she dared to say that she looked as good as the goddess Athene. Outraged, Athene turned Medusa's hair into snakes, her teeth into tusks and her hands into cold metal. Athene's final curse? Making Medusa's eyes turn men to stone. No-one would look at her now!

Hiss!

Spit!

Look at me when I'm talking to you!

Vital statistics

Name: Gorgon
Appearance: Very ugly: staring eyes, lolling tongue, ghastly grin
Size: Tall woman
Armed with: Snakes, tusks, bronze hands, golden wings
Home: Ancient Greece
Powers: Deadly gaze

You wouldn't want to know this:

Just one drop of Medusa's blood could kill. It was also used as powerful – but dangerous – medicine.

Be prepared!
Always expect the very worst

Aha! Gotcha!

Mirror, mirror

How can you kill a Gorgon without being turned to stone? Greek hero Perseus used his shield as a mirror so his eyes wouldn't meet Medusa's gaze, and he cut off her head!

Awful warning

The Greek goddess Athene wore Medusa's head on the front of her armour. It sent out an awful warning: 'I'm mighty and dangerous! Keep away!' Gorgon heads were carved on Greek temples, too, to stop evil spirits entering.

What's in a name?

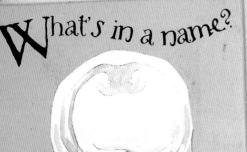

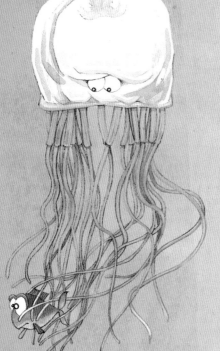

Some kinds of jellyfish have the name 'Medusa' because their long, trailing tentacles look like her snaky hair.

Don't look now!

Like Medusa, the Basilisk killed with a single glance. A very strange creature, it was hatched by a rooster from a serpent's egg, spat fire, and trailed poisonous slime.

Cluck!

No 59

Vampire

Dead but undead! Vampires cannot rest in peace, but haunt the world of the living, longing for fresh blood. Greed and violence are their only pleasures; they do not care how many they devour. Loathed and feared, they are outcasts forever – unless they are caught and killed (again!) in horrid and revolting ways.

Sinister cloak, like bat's wings

Mwahahaha!

Come closer! Very close! There's nothing to fear...

Vital statistics

Name: Vampire

Appearance: Deathly pale (or dark red); burning eyes, hairy palms

Size: From thin and hungry to bloated and swollen

Armed with: Fangs, claws, sinister smile

Home: Primarily Eastern Europe, but also worldwide

Powers: Bloodsucker!

You wouldn't want to know this:

Just one bite from a vampire will make you a vampire too.

Be prepared!
Always expect the very worst

Evil omen

Roman myths told how the Strix (screech owl) was once a woman, but she ate human flesh and blood, and became a vampire bird.

Screeeeech!

Seeing the Strix brought bad luck.

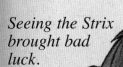

Vampire-proof?

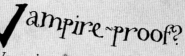

Vampires hate garlic and can't cross running water. The best advice? Don't let them near enough to kiss – or bite – you!

Worldwide horror

Vampire myths come from many lands. In Mexico, the Aztec Cihuateotl (Night Demon) stole children, sent madness and drank blood.

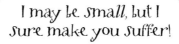

I may be small, but I sure make you suffer!

Mighty Bite!

Vampires are not the only creatures to suck blood. Tiny insects, such as moquitoes and bed-bugs (*pictured right*), also feast on it. Their bites itch, bleed and spread dangerous diseases. Ugh!

Itch!

193

Nº 90

Dragon

Marvel or monster? The dragon is both. Its size, strength and wisdom give it great powers to help or do harm. In Chinese myths, dragons mostly guard and guide – though they are awesomely awful when angry. Elsewhere in the world, dragons mean danger. They snatch and swallow victims, and their fiery breath destroys whole kingdoms. They also smell foul!

Chinese dragon

Roar!

Vital statistics

Name: Dragon (Chinese)

Appearance: Snake with legs

Size: Small as a silkworm, big as the world

Armed with: Sharp teeth and claws

Home: Up among rainclouds in the sky

Powers: Control the weather; guard emperors; become invisible; glow in the dark.

You wouldn't want to know this:

Angry dragons send disastrous tsunamis and floods.

Be prepared!
Always expect the very worst

Devil in disguise

Outside China, dragons are fierce, cruel devils. They delight in evil, and kill to win hoards of golden treasure.

It's mine! All mine!

Many-headed monster

Greek myths tell how hero Heracles fought the Hydra, a hundred-headed dragon. As he sliced heads off with his sword, more grew to replace them.

Hisss!

Spit!

Dragon of doom

Jormungandr, the World Serpent, appears in myths from Viking lands. He wraps himself round the world, holding his tail in his mouth. When he lets go, the world will end!

Grrr!

England's hero?

George, the patron saint of England, is famous for killing a dragon. But his story is a myth, in praise of courage. George probably never lived – but nor did dragons!

Stab!

Murky Mysteries

Paranormal experiences, strange curses and disappearing ships. You'll be scratching your head and screaming in fright!

№ 91

Lonely giants

We're Moai (honoured ancestors). There are 887 of us.

The year is 1722. The place, the Pacific Ocean. Nervously, Dutch sailors scramble ashore – the first Europeans to reach the island. But stop! What's that? Who are they? Rows of huge stone giants line the shore, towering above them. All around is bleak wasteland with no trees.

Who built them? How? What for?

Vital statistics

Name: Rapa Nui (Easter Island)
Location: Pacific Ocean, 4,000 km west of Santiago, Chile
Date: c.1600–1800
Mystery: Collapse of civilisation, death of inhabitants
Probable explanation: Environmental disaster caused by cutting down trees.

You wouldn't want to know this:

The Easter Islanders grew so hungry that they fought – and ate – each other.

Kon-Tiki

In 1955–1956, Norwegian adventurer Thor Heyerdahl sailed his raft *Kon-Tiki* from South America to one of the islands near Easter Island. He thought that the islands' first settlers had arrived that way – but scientists now believe this is unlikely.

Be prepared!
Always expect the very worst

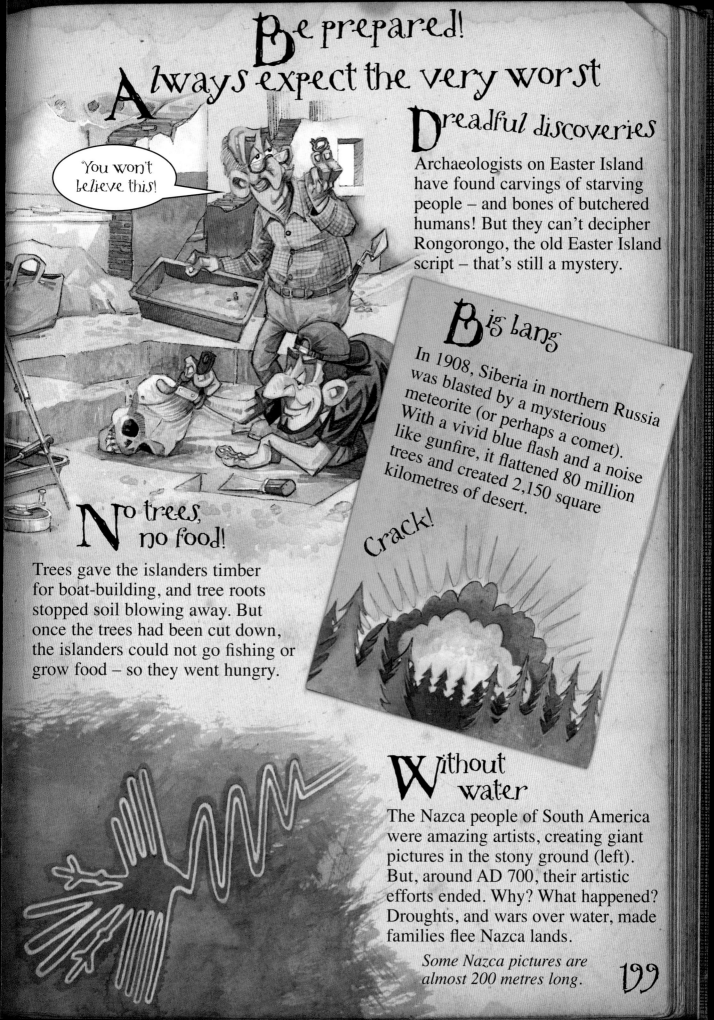

You won't believe this!

Dreadful discoveries

Archaeologists on Easter Island have found carvings of starving people – and bones of butchered humans! But they can't decipher Rongorongo, the old Easter Island script – that's still a mystery.

Big bang

In 1908, Siberia in northern Russia was blasted by a mysterious meteorite (or perhaps a comet). With a vivid blue flash and a noise like gunfire, it flattened 80 million trees and created 2,150 square kilometres of desert.

Crack!

No trees, no food!

Trees gave the islanders timber for boat-building, and tree roots stopped soil blowing away. But once the trees had been cut down, the islanders could not go fishing or grow food – so they went hungry.

Without water

The Nazca people of South America were amazing artists, creating giant pictures in the stony ground (left). But, around AD 700, their artistic efforts ended. Why? What happened? Droughts, and wars over water, made families flee Nazca lands.

Some Nazca pictures are almost 200 metres long.

199

Nᵒ 92

Bodies in the snow

I t's bitterly cold, and you've joined a rescue party searching for nine young student skiers who have mysteriously disappeared. Ah! There's their tent, but it's ripped open! And way over there are partly clothed bodies (with burnt hands!), frozen to death as they crawled through the snow. Later, you learn that more bodies have been found, with horrific injuries – a smashed skull, crushed ribs, and a missing tongue.

Vital statistics

Name: Dyatlov Pass incident
Location: A pass (lower slope between high peaks) in the Ural Mountains, Russia
Date: 1959
Mystery: Violent death of nine young skiers

Probable explanation: Maybe an avalanche, but no-one knows for sure

You wouldn't want to know this:

The students' dead bodies were said to have turned bright orange. Their hair had gone grey overnight. The night the students died, strange flashing lights were seen in the sky.

The temperature at Dyatlov Pass was way below freezing: −25°C or lower.

Be prepared!
Always expect the very worst

Murdered by a monster?

Traditional tales told of huge, hairy monsters that lurked in the mountains. Had one of these wild giants killed the skiers? Probably not – there were no monster footprints. Hypothermia is more likely.

Cold kills!

Look out for these signs of hypothermia (dangerously low body temperature):

- Shivering, goose bumps
- Hands and feet numb
- Sickness, blurred vision
- Feeling strangely warm
- Clumsiness and confusion
- Violent shaking, very pale
- Dazed, then unconscious – death follows.

Danger zone

When examined after death, the skiers' clothes showed high levels of atomic radiation. Had they strayed into a deadly secret weapon-testing zone?

Boom!

Deadly rays!

Innocent explanation

Mutilated bodies are always mysterious and disturbing. When dead cattle with missing tongues were found in the USA around 1960, farmers blamed spacemen, or vandals. In fact, the soft flesh had been eaten by scavenging birds and animals.

No 93
Deadly dancing

Here we go! Here we go! Here we go! Look, here come the dancers – wild, bloodstained, exhausted. Respectable men, women and children, dancing through the city streets. Yes, dancing until they drop dead! It's some sort of mass panic, caused by the troubled times they live in. They fear disease and war and famine, and feel very guilty for their sins.

Vital statistics

Name: Dancing plague
Location: Europe
Date: Around 1400–1600
Mystery: Why dance to death?

Probable explanation: Mass panic

You wouldn't want to know this:

Dancers leaped and swayed until their feet were raw and bloody, then ran around 'like wild beasts'.

I'm doomed! I fear Hell!

Our world is coming to an end!

My feet are killing me.

Be prepared!
Always expect the very worst

Poison fungus on grain

Miaow!

Mass panic

Deadly diseases, such as bubonic plague, caused panic. Fearing sudden death, victims ran wild, collapsed, or had hysterics. Natural poisons also caused strange symptoms – scary visions, twitching limbs – but rarely led to dancing.

Aaargh!

Bubo (deadly plague swelling)

Hisss!

No, Sister!

In the past, many Europeans believed in witchcraft and magic. This sometimes led to very strange behaviour – even among good, holy people. In 1491, Spanish nuns began to crawl and climb like cats, believing that they had been possessed (taken over) by devils.

Dance – and disappear!

Traditional tales tell how the Pied Piper of Hamelin saved the citizens from a plague of rats in 1284. When they would not pay him, he played his pipe again. This time, all the town's children (save two*) danced after him into a mysterious cave. They were never seen again.

*Some say that only one was left.

And all because of little old me!

203

№ 94
Wild child

Poor Victor! His life was tragic. No-one knew where he came from, but one day he was found in the woods, eating roots and acorns. About 12 years old, he was naked and filthy dirty. He could not talk, but sniffed at his captors like a dog. They took him to the big city, where experts tried – and mostly failed – to teach him 'civilised' behaviour. He died aged just 40 years old.

Vital statistics

Name: Victor, The Wild Boy of Aveyron
Location: France
Date: 1800
Mystery: Boy living wild in the woods

Probable explanation: Victor had mental problems, and had been thrown out (to die) by adults

You wouldn't want to know this:

Like any other wild creature, Victor was not house-trained. Slowly, he had to learn to use a lavatory.

Be prepared!
Always expect the very worst

fierce but famous

Legend has it that Romulus and Remus were nursed by a wolf, and grew up fierce and quarrelsome, like wild beasts. They built a great city, but Romulus killed Remus. Today, the city (Rome, the capital of Italy) is still named after him.

Angels or devils?

Around 1800, scholars were keen to study children's behaviour. Some said that children were naturally wild, like Victor. Others said children were born good, but learned to be bad by copying adults around them.

I wonder who was right...

Better than human?

In The Jungle Book (1894), British writer Rudyard Kipling told stories about a wild boy in the Indian jungle and his animal friends. Most of Kipling's creatures were kinder and wiser than humans.

The horrible truth

In real life, wild animals are not nice to children. That's why traditional tales like 'Red Riding Hood' were invented. Such stories warn children not to stray into wild places – and meet with deadly danger.

All the better to EAT you with, my dear!

№ 95

Invisible!

Just imagine! It's wartime, and you're in a US Navy dockyard. There's a small ship next to you – the USS Eldridge – and suddenly it disappears in a flash of weird light! Ten seconds later, it slowly comes back. Some of the crew are welded to its hull, some have gone mad with fear. Others have vanished!

Vital statistics

Name: The Philadelphia Experiment
Date: 1943
Place: Philadelphia, USA
Mystery: Strange science: an invisible ship

Probable explanation: Wartime worries; crazy story

You wouldn't want to know this:

At the time when the 'Philadelphia Experiment' story was created, many people feared that new, scientific weapons would soon blow the world to bits.

I've got time-travel sickness!

I've been teleported!

Be prepared!
Always expect the very worst

Science fiction

In 1957, scribbled notes arrived at US Navy headquarters. The writer claimed that scientists had been trying to make the USS *Eldridge* invisible – but, because the experiment had gone wrong, it had been kept top secret. The story was completely untrue – but millions believed it!

Changing waves

In naval dockyards like the one at Philadelphia, warships were electrically treated so that underwater mines could not detect them. This 'de-gaussing' changed the pattern of magnetic waves around the ships' hulls. But they did not disappear!

These are strange orders, Captain! First we turn to green fog, then we disappear!

Military mysteries

Although there was no Philadephia Experiment, the US Army did investigate strange science. For example, in the 1970s soldiers tried to use mind-power to kill. They practised by staring at goats!

Einstein's ideas

Albert Einstein (1879–1955) was the greatest scientist of the 20th century. His theories suggest that it might be possible to distort (bend or stretch) space, light and time. Perhaps they inspired the story?

$E = mc^2$

I surrender!

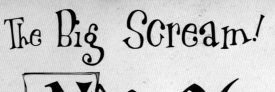

№ 96

Stormy waters

You've probably heard of it – the famous Bermuda Triangle. Hundreds of ships and planes are rumoured to have vanished there, without warning, most mysteriously!

But in 1975, careful calculations proved that there were no more shipwrecks or plane crashes there than in any other busy transport zone.

USA

Bermuda

Florida

Puerto Rico

Caribbean Sea

Vital statistics

Name: Bermuda Triangle
Date: 1945–1975
Place: Sea between south-east USA and Bermuda
Mystery: Disappearing ships and planes

Probable explanation: Imagined by journalists, keen to sell exciting stories

You wouldn't want to know this:

The Bermuda Triangle was also known as The Devil's Triangle. That was meant to show how scary it was!

The real mystery is why people still say the Bermuda Triangle is dangerous!

Don't spoil it! We all like a good story!

208

Be prepared!
Always expect the very worst

Alien attack?

The Bermuda Triangle was first mentioned in stories about the doomed Flight 19: in 1945, five US Navy planes vanished mysteriously. Probably, their pilots made a fatal mistake and crashed into the sea – but some writers blamed space invaders.

Natural hazards?

Other writers said that hurricanes, wild waves, fast currents and giant bubbles of natural gas from the seabed had wrecked ships sailing across the Bermuda Triangle. This was possible, but could not be proved.

Hurricanes often strike Bermuda.

Whoosh!

Into the unknown?

Disappearances have always made good stories. In AD 117, it was said, the Roman 9th Legion marched out of York, England, and vanished! In fact, the Legion really was overpowered by enemies – but that happened 15 years later, and in the Middle East!

After all, it's a great tale!

Roar!

Does it really matter who destroyed us?

The Big Scream!

The mummy's curse

The magnificent golden treasures found in Pharaoh Tutankhamun's tomb caused a worldwide sensation when they were discovered in 1922. The death soon after of Lord Carnarvon, who had paid for the excavations, became almost as famous. People linked the two events, and declared, 'A mysterious curse killed him!'

Vital statistics

Name: Curse of Tutankhamun
Date: 1922 onwards
Place: Valley of the Kings, Egypt
Mystery: Did an ancient curse kill archaeologists who discovered Tutankhamun's tomb?

Probable solution: Lord Carnarvon's death was a coincidence – the curse was just an exotic, exciting rumour!

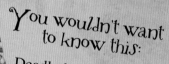

You wouldn't want to know this:

Deadly bacteria and poisonous gases are often found in ancient tombs – even today.

Can you see anything?

Wonderful things!

Be prepared!
Always expect the very worst

Unlucky treasures?

Great wealth made onlookers envious. Sometimes they may have felt like cursing the rich. But many curses were invented – by merchants selling treasures. A story of a mysterious curse won publicity, raised prices, and added a thrill to business deals.

Since 1908, it's been claimed that the beautiful blue Hope Diamond is cursed and brings disaster. Today's value? £200 million!

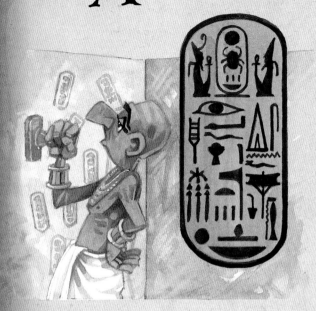

Life after death

Magic spells and religious sayings decorated the entrance to many Egyptian tombs. But they were not curses. Most were designed to help dead people survive for ever in the Afterlife.

The real reason

There was no curse! Lord Carnarvon had been in poor health for many years. He died from a mosquito bite that became infected, and poisoned him.

How, why, who?

Mighty, mysterious and very, very old, the pyramids in Egypt puzzled people for centuries. Some said aliens built them, or a vanished superhuman race. Actually, Egypt's farmers built the pyramids, using muscle power and simple tools of stone and copper.

Now that is amazing.

N̶o 93

House of horror

Tourists flocked to Amityville to see the mysterious house of horror.

First, it was a house of tragedy. In 1974, a young man living there murdered his parents, brothers and sisters. A year later, a new family moved in – but fled in terror just 28 days later. They claimed they were driven out by horrific ghosts and demons. Was the house evil and haunted, as they said? Or had they imagined everything – then sought publicity for their story?

Vital statistics

Name: House of horror
Place: Amityville, Long Island, New York, USA
Date: 1975
Mystery: Ghastly haunted house

Probable explanation: A hoax

You wouldn't want to know this:

It was said that the youngest child of the new arrivals at Amityville was haunted by an evil pig-faced monster!

Do you get the feeling it's looking at us?

Be prepared!
Always expect the very worst

Very, very nasty

The new family claimed to be pestered by strange sounds, vile smells, swarms of flies, and sickly green slime. They spoke of red staring eyes in the darkness, demon footprints, and much more. A best-selling book and nine films were based on their story.

Unquiet spirits?

Had mysterious ghosts led the young man to murder, and then haunted the new family? Was the Amityville house built on an old, evil site, where Native Americans once died? Absolutely not – although some people thought so. History shows that no such place existed.

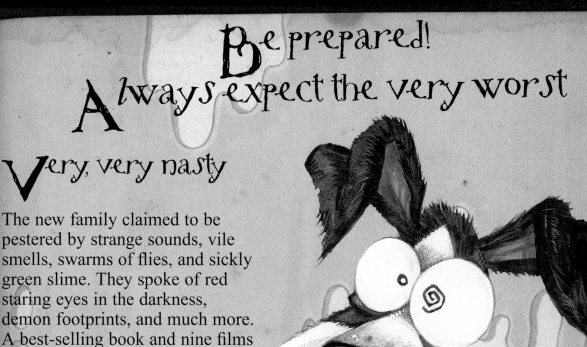

Oddly enough, I slept through some of these horrors. Sometimes I wonder if they really happened...

Who's next for the Ripper?

Worse than human?

In 1888, London was shocked by a series of brutal murders. The killer was never discovered, but was nicknamed 'Jack the Ripper'. Some said that he was not a man, but a monster. Like tourists at Amityville, who believed in demons, they did not like to think that humans could be so evil.

Nº 99

The Mary Celeste

Ship ahoy! There she is! It's the *Mary Celeste*, sailing through calm seas with her heavy, dangerous cargo. But hey, that's strange! She's not steering straight, and her sails are flapping wildly. I can't see anyone on deck. It looks as though they've all abandoned her!

> She's carrying barrels of alcohol.

> You have to be careful with that. It can explode.

Vital statistics

Name: *Mary Celeste*
Date: 1872
Place: Atlantic Ocean, near Portugal
Mystery: Empty ship, no sign of crew

Probable explanation: The crew abandoned ship because they feared sinking, or an explosion.

You wouldn't want to know this:

The captain's two-year-old daughter was on board. She vanished along with the others.

Be prepared!
Always expect the very worst

Whooosh!

Washed away?

Rescuers found water a metre deep in the *Mary Celeste's* hold. Above, everything was soaking wet, from the captain's bed to the ship's compass.
Was the ship swamped by freak waves or a whirling waterspout? No-one knows!

The flying Dutchman

Another sea mystery! Many sailors claim to have seen this ghostly ship and its haunted captain. Always, they're a warning of bad luck and foul weather. The 'Dutchman' appears suddenly, bathed in an eerie glow. Its story may perhaps be based on real-life mirages.

> I'm doomed! My punishment is to sail the seas forever!

A watery grave?

No-one knows what happened to the *Mary Celeste's* sailors. Without witnesses or evidence, their fate remains a mystery. Probably, they climbed overboard into the lifeboat. Then they either died of cold, hunger and thirst, or drowned.

> We're safer here. That ship's dangerous!

No 100

Alien invaders

Tall and green? Short and silver? Friendly, peculiar, dangerous? Who knows what alien invaders might look like? Except in films, on TV and in computer games, no-one has ever seen one. Unless, perhaps, you believe the mysterious stories told about a ranch at Roswell, USA. There, a farmhand thought he might have found strange wreckage – from a spaceship!

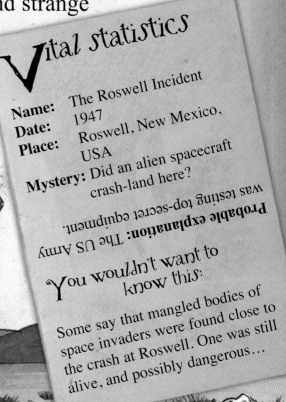

Vital statistics

Name: The Roswell Incident
Date: 1947
Place: Roswell, New Mexico, USA
Mystery: Did an alien spacecraft crash-land here?

Probable explanation: The US Army was testing top-secret equipment.

You wouldn't want to know this:

Some say that mangled bodies of space invaders were found close to the crash at Roswell. One was still alive, and possibly dangerous…

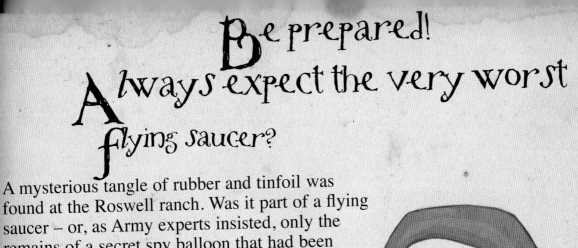

Be prepared!
Always expect the very worst

flying saucer?

A mysterious tangle of rubber and tinfoil was found at the Roswell ranch. Was it part of a flying saucer – or, as Army experts insisted, only the remains of a secret spy balloon that had been tracking enemy weapons?

foo fighters

In the 1940s, calm, trained, professional pilots saw mysterious balls of light that glowed bright, raced through the sky and disappeared. Nicknamed 'foo fighters', they have never been fully explained. They may have been rocket-flares, or a kind of lightning.

A tragic end?

The mysterious Roswell 'aliens' may have been dummies, used by aircraft designers to measure the impact of crash-landings. Or, tragically, they may have been the crew of a US Air Force plane, killed when its fuel tanks exploded.

Humans? No, I don't believe in them.

GLOSSARY

Amphibian A vertebrate that lives on land or in water and lays eggs.

Ancient Referring to something that existed before the Middle Ages, the 5th century AD.

Arachnid An arthropod (animal with a hard outer skeleton) that has a head, a body and eight legs.

Archaeologist A scientist who studies the remains of past civilisations.

Armada A large group of warships.

Astrolabe A navigation instrument used to measure the position of the sun above the horizon.

Bacteria Tiny living things which can only be seen with a microscope. Some of them can cause disease.

Bankrupt Having no money.

Barbary Coast An old name for the coast of North Africa.

Bipedal Standing on two feet.

Body snatcher Someone who steals dead bodies from their graves. Also called a grave robber.

Booty Stolen goods.

Bubonic plague A disease which killed millions of people in medieval Europe. It is spread by diseased fleas that live on rats.

Cabin boy A young boy working as a servant or trainee sailor on board ship.

Calico Lightweight cotton cloth.

Cartilaginous fish A fish with a skeleton of bendy tissue (gristle) rather than bone.

Corsairs Licensed raiders in the Mediterranean Sea and North Atlantic Ocean.

Dhow A cargo ship with three masts, a high, curving hull and triangular sails, built to sail in the Indian Ocean.

GLOSSARY

Dividers A mathematical instrument used to measure distances on a map or a globe.

Docks A place where ships can be tied up next to dry land.

Drought A lack of water.

Dysentery An infectious disease that causes serious diarrhoea. It can be fatal if modern medicines are not available.

Excavation The process of digging into the ground to look for remains of past civilisations.

Extinct No longer existing or living.

Feud A long-standing argument between two groups or families.

Fossil The buried remains of a plant or animal, turned into stone by a natural process over thousands or millions of years.

Galleon A large cargo ship, built for long-distance voyages. It had a deep hull, three masts and large rectangular sails.

Habitat A plant or animal's natural place to live.

Heir A person who inherits (or will inherit) a title or property from someone who has died.

Hieroglyphics A system of writing used by the ancient Egyptians, especially for sacred texts.

Hoax A trick played on people to make them believe something that isn't true.

Hostages People held against their will whose captors want to exchange their lives for a ransom, which is often a large sum of money.

Human rights Rights such as safety, justice and freedom, belonging equally to all human beings.

GLOSSARY

Inquisitive Liking to ask a lot of questions.

Invertebrate An animal without a backbone.

Larva (plural: larvae) An immature animal that will change into another form when it becomes an adult.

Legend A traditional tale that contains bits of history but may not be completely true.

Livestock Animals raised specifically to provide people with labour, food or fur.

Looting Stealing from places which have been damaged by natural disasters or war.

Malaria A disease carried by mosquitoes, which can be fatal if modern medicines are not available.

Mammal A vertebrate that gives birth to live young and suckles them.

Measles A viral infection that causes a rash, inflammation and, in the past, death. Today it can be prevented by vaccination.

Oracle In ancient history, a person who was said to speak for the gods, often predicting the future.

Pandemic The fast spread of a disease across many countries.

Pilgrim A person who makes a long journey to a place of religious importance.

Prehistoric The period of time before recorded history.

Primitive At an early stage of evolution.

Prohibition A period in United States history when it was illegal to produce or sell alcohol (from 1920 to 1933).

GLOSSARY

Radiocarbon dating A method of finding out how old things are by measuring the amount of radioactive carbon that they contain. It works only on animal or plant materials.

Ransom The amount of money that a hostage-taker wants in return for their hostages.

Renaissance A period that saw a great revival of art in Europe (from the 14th to the 16th centuries).

Reptile A cold-blooded vertebrate that breathes air and has skin covered with scales.

Revolutionary A person who plans or takes part in a plot to overthrow a ruler or a government.

Sacrifice A living creature that is killed in order to please or to calm the gods.

Scavenger An animal that searches for decaying flesh for food.

Sub-tropical Belonging to the regions immediately north and south of the tropics.

Tropical Belonging to the tropics – the region between the Tropic of Cancer north of the Equator and the Tropic of Capricorn, south of the equator.

Tsunami A huge and destructive wave of water.

Vertebrate An animal with a backbone.

INDEX

INDEX